T0012504

CULTURE SMART!

ETHIOPIA

THE ESSENTIAL GUIDE TO CUSTOMS & CULTURE

SARAH HOWARD

KUPERARD

"The real voyage of discovery consists not in seeking new landscapes, but in having new eyes."

Adapted from Marcel Proust, *Remembrance of Things Past*.

ISBN 978 1 78702 264 5

British Library Cataloguing in Publication Data
A CIP catalogue entry for this book is available
from the British Library

First published in Great Britain
by Kuperard, an imprint of Bravo Ltd
59 Hutton Grove, London N12 8DS
Tel: +44 (0) 20 8446 2440
www.culturesmart.co.uk
Inquiries: publicity@kuperard.co.uk

Design Bobby Birchall
Printed in Turkey by Elma Basım

The Culture Smart! series is continuing to expand.
All Culture Smart! guides are available as e-books, and many
as audio books. For further information and latest titles visit
www.culturesmart.co.uk

SARAH HOWARD is a botanical artist and writer who spent her childhood in Kenya. After graduating in African History and Social Anthropology from the School of Oriental and African Studies, University of London, she became a journalist and researcher for two Anglican agencies, and undertook the archiving of the Leakey family papers in Kenya. She continues to offer archival advice on private collections pertaining to East Africa. Since 1989 she has commuted between Scotland and Ethiopia. Turning her interest to plants, she trained in botanical illustration at the Royal Botanic Garden Edinburgh and helped to illustrate the seminal *Flora of Ethiopia and Eritrea* (Addis Ababa University). She is currently working on painting portraits of Ethiopia's endemic plants.

COVID-19

The coronavirus pandemic of 2020 affected millions of people around the world, causing unprecedented social and economic disruption. As the impact of this global crisis continues to unfold, in many countries social norms are being challenged, and enduring changes will be reflected in future editions of Culture Smart! titles.

CONTENTS

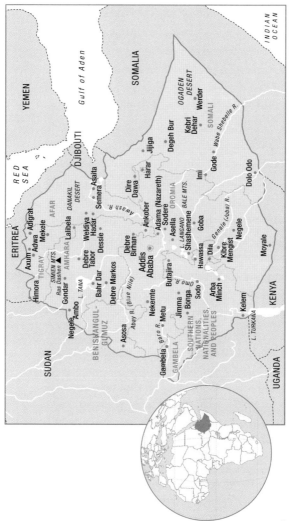

Set in Africa, but not wholly African; an isolated nation, yet receptive to the outside world; hierarchical and conservative, yet innovative and desirous of modernity; conformist as a people, and yet fiercely independent as individuals—the Ethiopian identity defies definition. No sooner have you made a generalization than you realize it does not apply to some other part of the country. This is because Ethiopia was once an empire, made up of many different peoples and cultures.

Ethiopia exists simultaneously in different time periods. Its people, when they come upon something new that might work to their advantage, will embrace it and find ways to improve on it. But they see no reason to change something they have learned to live with over the centuries. Modern democracy has been slow to take hold, given the strong historical antecedents of an imperial past, and Ethiopian bureaucracy can baffle both foreigner and local alike, but they do not question it; instead, they do what they have always done—work round it creatively.

All Ethiopians are proud of their history. They are so proud, in fact, that some outsiders see them as condescending. They resist foreign ownership of their assets, sometimes at the cost of economic development, and they resent outside interference. They are proud of being the only African country that fought off attempted conquest and colonization.

Outwardly formal and courteous, Ethiopians present themselves with gravitas, expressed in polite bows to whomever they may meet. Their courtesy is born of the consciousness of being members of a multilingual and multicultural polity, where in order to get on, people have to respect each other. When foreigners experience this, it is not because they are seen as superior, but because they are being treated to the same politeness as an Ethiopian from a different region.

Ethiopians also have a great sense of fun and are capable of great wit, with a penchant for puns and slapstick. This book goes a short way toward introducing you to the Ethiopian peoples. Take an interest in Ethiopia's culture and history, and you will be warmly welcomed by your hosts.

Official Name	Federal Democratic Republic of Ethiopia	The older name Abyssinia properly refers only to the Amhara and Tigray regions.
Capital City	Addis Ababa	Pop. 4.8 million (est.) Alt. 7,870 ft (2,400 m)
Administrative Regions and Capitals	Afar (Semera); Amhara (Bahr Dar); Benishangul-Gumuz (Asosa); Gambela (Gambela); Harari (Harar); Oromia (Finfinne/ Addis Ababa); Somali (Jijiga); Sidama (Hawassa); Southern Nations, Nationalities and Peoples (Hawassa); Tigray (Mekele). Addis Ababa and Dire Dawa are chartered cities with the same status as the regions. Addis Ababa is the country's capital, capital of a region, and a chartered city.	
Official Federal Languages	Amharic is the official state language. English is the official foreign language.	Each region has its official language. Some use the Latin alphabet, others a script derived from the Ge'ez language.
Area	435,000 sq. miles (1.14 million sq. km)	
Borders	Eritrea, Djibouti, Somalia, Kenya, Sudan, South Sudan	
Climate	Temperate to alpine in the mountains; tropical in the lowlands. Varies with altitude and aspect	Two main seasons: dry from Oct. to May, and wet from June to Sept. Poss. "short rains" in March and April
Economy	Agriculture	Approx. 70% of people earn their living from the land.
Currency	Ethiopian Birr (ETB), divided into 100 Santim (centimes)	Coins of 1, 5, 10, 25, and 50 santim; banknotes for 1, 5, 10, 50, and 100 Birr

Population	114 million (est.) Median age 19.5 years	Average children per woman: 4.3. Infant mortality: 39 per 1,000
Ethnic Diversity from Outside the Horn of Africa	There is a large population of Italians, Greeks, and Armenians, mostly in Addis Ababa.	There are also communities of Yemenis, Saudi Arabians and, more recently, Chinese.
Main Linguistic Groups	Semitic (Amhara, Tigray and Gurage), Cushitic (Oromo, Somali and Afar), Nilotic (Nuer and Anuak)	There are 83 major languages. Amharinya and Tigrinya are the major Semitic languages; Oromifa and Somali are the main Cushitic languages.
Religion	Ethiopian Orthodox Christianity and Sunni Islam are the two major religions.	Also Protestant and Catholic Churches, and animistic beliefs in the south
Government	Democratically elected federal government, with elected regional governments	Local government consists of *woredas* (districts), town councils, and *kebeles* (parishes).
Electricity	220 volts, 50 Hz	Plugs are generally two-pronged.
Internet Domain	.et	
Telephone	Country code 251 Cell phone numbers within Ethiopia begin 091.	To call out of the country, dial 00 followed by the country code.
Calendar	The Ethiopian Calendar used in addition to the Western (Gregorian) calendar.	The Middle Eastern clock is also used in Ethiopia, and begins at sunrise, or 6:00 a.m.
Time Zone	GMT plus 3 hours, all year round	

CHAPTER ONE

LAND & PEOPLE

GEOGRAPHY

Ethiopia rises from arid lowlands to lofty mountain towers: a landlocked country that sits on a well-watered mountain plateau in the Horn of Africa. Its lowlands border on Eritrea, Djibouti, and Somalia to the north and east; Kenya to the south; and Sudan and South Sudan to the west. This "island" in the middle of desert largely dictates Ethiopia's natural resources, human settlement, and history.

With its cooler temperatures the highland plateau, rising from 5,000 to 10,000 feet (1,500 to 3,000 meters), carries the bulk of the population, provides the best agricultural land, and can generate as much hydroelectricity as Ethiopia needs. Limits are, however, imposed by its rugged terrain. A complex structure of metamorphic, sedimentary, volcanic, and intrusive rocks is riven by a huge block fault averaging thirty miles wide (fifty kilometers)

Gheralta Mountains on the Hawzien Plane, Tigray.

in the form of the Great Rift Valley. Smaller faults, particularly to the northwest of the Rift Valley, have created vast canyons, of which the Blue Nile gorge is the deepest. In the north the mountains rise to the peculiar, perpendicular-sided, flat-topped peaks of the Simien Mountains of more than 14,000 feet (4,300 meters). The highlands to the southeast of the Rift are gentler in character, but rise almost as high in the Bale Mountains, with the magnificent south-facing Harenna escarpment. The whole area continues to be unstable, with small earthquakes common, and hot springs prevalent.

Aptly described as "the reservoir of Africa," Ethiopia has river systems upon which its near neighbors in Somalia, Sudan, and Egypt are particularly reliant. Draining the northern mountains is the Abay (Blue Nile) River and its

tributaries, which supply two-thirds of the Nile's water north of Khartoum. To the south, the Wabe Shebelle and Genale rivers flow to the Indian Ocean through Somalia. The Awash flows into desert near Djibouti, and the Omo flows into landlocked Lake Turkana. Many of these rivers are dammed to generate hydroelectricity.

The Rift Valley itself widens out in the north to the harsh Danakil desert, where the hottest annual mean temperature on Earth has been recorded, and drops away in the south to the desert of northern Kenya. In between, the altitude rises to about 5,500 feet (1,700 meters). A series of lakes along the Rift Valley floor provides irrigation where the water is fresh, though many are saline. From the plateau the land gives way to the Ogaden desert bordering Somalia in the east, and, to the west, humid lowlands bordering Sudan.

CLIMATE

Ethiopia's generally high altitude offsets the effects of its position in the tropics, just to the north of the Equator. Temperatures are cool at night and the main rains are usually very heavy. In the lowland fringes the climate can be uncertain and is a cause of food insecurity. The main rains (*kremt*) begin at the end of June in Addis Ababa, slightly later in Tigray, and peter out during September. Many foreigners choose this time to leave the country, but it is vital planting time for Ethiopian farmers. The southern part of the country is influenced by the monsoons blowing in from the Indian Ocean. The fickle short rains (*belg*) around Easter make another planting possible, but as elsewhere the climate

Landscape around Mount Abune Yosef in the Amhara region—one of the highest mountains in Ethiopia.

is changing with noticeably less precipitation and warmer average temperatures.

Ethiopians refer to three zones: a cool zone (*dega*) in the highest mountains, where daytime temperatures range from freezing to 60°F (16°C) in the hot months; the temperate *weyna dega* zone has temperatures from 60°–86°F (16°–30°C), where a sweater is needed at night; and the *kolla* zone, lying below 5,000 feet (1,500 meters) in the deserts and at the bottoms of big river gorges, where daytime temperatures average 80°F (27°C).

FLORA AND FAUNA

Humans have modified greatly the natural landscape in Ethiopia, particularly in the north. Primary forests have been much reduced and the Rift Valley is badly degraded. Yet there is much to observe and to protect. As an "island" ecosystem, Ethiopia has developed both a specialist natural life, particularly in the highest and driest areas, as well as a high degree of biodiversity, notably in economically important food crops such as cereals and coffee. The Bale Mountains are central to the flora hotspot known as Somali-Masai (Horn of Africa). The Rift Valley, with its lakes, is an important migration route for birds, and a number of national parks and reserves exist to protect unique fauna.

The Australian eucalyptus tree (*Eucalyptus globulus*) dominates the eye around Addis Ababa, and every other town and village, and is an essential source of fuel. It is, though, only one among over 7,000 higher plant species existing in Ethiopia, of which about 12 percent are endemic. Vegetation zones broadly follow Ethiopia's complex topography. These range from semidesert scrub, through acacia woodland, to moist montane forest—in which coffee still grows wild—or dry montane forest containing magnificent trees, such as the *Podocarpus falcatus* and the medicinally important *Hagenia abyssinica*. Vivid red *Acanthus sennii* grow along the roadsides in this zone, a striking plant endemic to Ethiopia. High in the alpine regions, where nightly frosts are a feature, there are plants well adapted to their environment, such as prickly clumps of the shrub *Helichrysum citrispinum* and the giant treelike *Lobelia rhynchopetalum*, whose old leaves protect its stem from freezing.

The Rift Valley lakes provide an important migration corridor between Eastern Europe and Southern Africa and, as a result, Ethiopia, together with Eritrea, is one of Africa's hot spots for bird-watching. There are over 850 known species of birds, including some 20 species endemic to Ethiopia, many of which are locally common and easy to spot. These include the Black-winged Lovebird (*Agapornis taranta*), found near water in cities, and the Thick-billed Raven (*Corvus crassirostris*) on the hills surrounding Addis Ababa.

Ethiopia is also home to more than 300 mammal species, of which some 55 are endemic. A number of national parks and conservation areas exist to protect these animals, but the pressures of a growing population and livestock make some of them difficult to sustain. The Ethiopian wolf (*Canis simensis*), easily seen in the Bale Mountains, with about four hundred in existence is the world's rarest canine.

Habitat loss, together with climate change, are major conservation issues facing the government of Ethiopia, together with the protection of forests to preserve rainfall.

PEOPLE

The Ethiopians derive from both African and Middle Eastern peoples and form several distinctive nations and tribes. In the west, tall Nilotic tribes straddle the border with Sudan. In the south and east are various Cushitic-speaking peoples, such as the clannish cattle-rearing Oromo who have migrated northward into the area, and nomadic camel-keeping Somalis who straddle the southeast border. In the north are Semitic-speaking and sedentary Amharas and Tigrayans who define the Christian heartland.

Cutting across these ethnic spatial divides are historically important elites based on aristocracy, church or court, creating class and hierarchy. Intermarriage is common in towns and where couples have encountered each other outside their home areas.

Eighty different languages are spoken in the country. Amharic is the working language of the federal government and is understood widely. It has its own script that, like Arabic, uses a system of phonetic consonants with extra markings for the vowels, but unlike Arabic is written from left to right. More recently, under devolved government, younger people in the Regions study their own vernacular first, English second, and usually also Amharic.

In more recent centuries, families from various European nationalities have made their way to Ethiopia and many of them have intermarried with Ethiopians. These include Greeks, Armenians, and Italians. A reverse migration has also occurred from the time of the Derg, when Ethiopians created their own diaspora—an estimated one million are living in the United States, and probably the same number again in Europe.

About two million people are added to the population each year, representing an approximate 2.5 percent growth per annum. Sixty percent of the estimated population of 113 million (2019) is under 25 years old. With so many new mouths to feed each year, the government is presented with a formidable challenge to its development policy.

REGIONS

Tigray

This region covers the highlands in the north of Ethiopia. It encompasses the ancient Kingdom of Axum, and was divided in the nineteenth century into part of what is now highland Eritrea and the southern area, which remained part of Ethiopia. The Christian faith and the language, Tigrinya, are common bonds both within Tigray and with the Eritreans across the border. There are rich tourist opportunities in historical centers such as Axum and the many clusters of rock-hewn churches around Tigray. Mekele, founded by Yohannes IV in the late nineteenth century, is the capital. Terracing and tree planting by community effort is rejuvenating badly degraded agricultural land in the region.

Amhara

This region covers the Amharic-speaking provinces of Gondar, Gojjam, Wollo, and North Shoa in the central highlands of Ethiopia, west of the Rift

Fasilides Castle, Gondar. Founded by Emperor Fasilides in the 17th century, the castle and surrounding fortress is a UNESCO World Heritage Site.

Valley. Its people are mostly Christian, but there are many Muslims—especially in Wollo, which borders the Rift Valley, where Muslim camel traders mix with highlanders at the big markets at the foot of the escarpment. Small-scale farming is generally practiced. The leafy, lakeside city of Bahr Dar by Lake Tana is capital of Amhara. Other main towns are Dessie in Wollo, Gondar in the north, and various ancient sites such as Ankober and Debre Tabor.

Afar

The Afar language, Islam, and camels bind the Afar Region, which covers the hot, arid lowlands to the east of the highland plateau. The Awash River flows through it providing the Afar region's only crop-producing potential, although the water never reaches the sea and peters out in a series of saline lakes near the Djibouti border. It is bound to its neighboring regions by trade and by nomads who bring their camels to grasslands in the higher areas during the dry season. The former capital, Asaita, is the center of a relatively well-irrigated area on the Awash River. The new capital is Semera.

Harar

This is the smallest region and surrounds the ancient walled city of Harar. Coffee and *chat* are the mainstays of the economy. Most people are Muslim, though there is one important Christian pilgrimage center, Kulubi Mariam, near Harar. Harar is an ancient Muslim site where a unique language called Adare is spoken.

People in the walled city of Harar.

Dire Dawa

One of two chartered cities (along with Addis Ababa),
Dire Dawa lies northwest of Harar on the Djibouti-
Addis Ababa railway. It is Ethiopia's second-largest
city and a major industrial and trading center. It has
an international airport, a major railway station, and
cosmopolitan inhabitants.

Somali Region

Peopled by ethnic Somalis and covering the Ogaden
desert, the Somali Region is probably the least
accessible to outsiders. All Muslim, mostly camel
keeping, watered only by the Genale (Juba) and Wabe
Shebelle rivers that a rise in the Bale Mountains, the

region borders on both orderly de facto independent
Somaliland (formerly British Somaliland) and
the disturbed state of Somalia (formerly Italian
Somaliland), which gives Ethiopia its greatest security
problem. Jijiga, to the east of Harar, is the main town.

Oromia

This is the largest of Ethiopia's regions and contains
all the various Oromo-speaking peoples, who are the
most populous ethnic group. It ranges from Shoa in
the north, to the Kenyan border in the south, and
most of western Ethiopia, including Wellega. Addis
Ababa is the capital, and it includes large towns such
as Debre Zeit, Jimma, Adama (also known by its
former name, Nazareth), and Asella. It includes the
Bale Mountains and most of the eastern side of the
Rift Valley. The Oromo language has diverse dialects
and the people are largely Muslim or Christian,
particularly of various Protestant denominations. All
types of agriculture are practiced, including nomadic
cattle keeping in the Rift Valley, coffee and sedentary
agriculture in the highlands, where the potential is
high with rich volcanic and well-watered soils.

Southern Nations, Nationalities, and Peoples (SNNP) Region

The sheer diversity of small linguistic groups, cultures,
and religions makes this area difficult to generalize
about. It covers the highlands on the western side of
the southern Rift Valley in the southwest of Ethiopia,
and includes important nations, such as: Gurage,

A group of women from the Hamer tribe.

centered on Butajira, in the Gurage Highlands;
Welayta, centered on Sodo; as well as small tribes
favored by tourists, such as the Mursi, Hamer, and
Konso. It also includes the coffee-bearing forests
around the town of Bonga, which is reached via
Jimma. Hawassa, on Lake Hawassa, is its capital and

Girls of the Mursi tribe.

is gateway to the important coffee-growing Sidamo area to the south. This area, too, is agriculturally rich in coffee and cattle, with important forests on the higher slopes of the Rift Valley scarps. Its peoples practice a mixture of religions, including mainly Protestant and Catholic Christianity, Islam, and paganism. Amharic is the working language. The largest component, Sidamo, voted in 2019 to be an autonomous region, and the Sidamo lakeside city, Hawassa, will be the shared capital of both Sidamo and SNNP.

Gambela
Centered on the town of Gambela on the Baro River, Gambela Region is low-lying, humid, and hot. Its people are mainly a mixture of nomadic cattle-keeping

Nuer and Anuak, a Nilo-Saharan language group, who straddle the border with southern Sudan. They are traditionally pagan, but recently there has been a surge of Protestant Christianity among them. The Baro River flows through Gambela, before becoming the Sobat in Sudan, and flowing into the White Nile. Gambela town was an important port trading with British Sudan.

Benishangul-Gumuz

This region to the northwest of Ethiopia, which straddles the Abay (Nile), was carved out of western Gojjam and northern Wellega. It is mostly highland, but dips down toward the Sudanese border. There are diverse peoples, ranging from the Berta, Gumuz, and Shinasha, who have more in common with the Sudanese, to large numbers of Amhara and Tigrayans, who were resettled during the Derg era, and Oromos. More than 60 percent of the land is forested, including bamboo, eucalyptus, and rubber and resin trees, which are important to the local economy. Asosa is the capital.

Addis Ababa

Addis Ababa is one of two chartered cities in Ethiopia with its own elected mayor and its own administrative structure. It is also the capital of the country, and by far the largest city, with more than four million people. It was founded in 1887 around hot springs, known as Finfinne, by Emperor Menelik II. His wife, the Empress Taitu, who enjoyed the hot springs, gave the name Addis Ababa ("new flower" in Amharic) to the emergent town. When local supplies of wood began to be exhausted, it

A view of Addis Ababa.

was the introduction of the eucalyptus tree in the 1890s that saved the capital from moving elsewhere. The city is surrounded by the Oromia Region.

Addis Ababa sprawls over several hills and ravines at a heady altitude ranging from 7,000–9,000 feet (2,100–2,700 meters). Five major road arteries radiate from the city to the regions, and Meskel Square, at the heart of the city, is where big national events take place. There is a rapidly growing financial center around the National Theatre, and the Bole area adjacent to the airport has become the place for affluent shopping malls and high value houses, with a nightlife to match. New ring roads and a city train line have both eased movement and caused dire congestion, with frequent blockages or road closures.

The Mercato is a huge market area and forms a distinct, mainly Muslim, community within the city. The various nationalities of Ethiopia mingle with long-established foreign communities, of which the Yemeni is by far the biggest. Trading and commerce in both traditional and new commodities, from hides to laptop computers, is based on relationships of trust that sometimes go back several generations.

Although areas of the city have traditional names and the modern names of the main streets appear on maps, they are not commonly recognized. It is more usual to find your way about by means of GPS or discuss local reference points, such as a church or an embassy, with a taxi driver.

A BRIEF HISTORY

The story of Ethiopia begins with the birth of humankind, and interplays with that of the Middle East. Nevertheless, its mountaintop position in Africa caused a unique Christian monarchy to develop in its heartland, providing the basis for a modern nation to adapt and change to twenty-first century norms.

The Cradle of Mankind

The story began millions of years ago when humans were beginning to take shape. The discovery in 1974 of Dinkenesh (also known as "Lucy"), *Australopithecus afarensis* (3.2 million years old) in the Rift Valley at Hadar, established Afar Region as an important area for the discovery of paleontological remains. In 1992, *Australopithecus ramidus* bones (4.4 million years old) were found, also in Afar. These seem to be a "missing link" between hominids and their immediate ancestors. Between 1997 and 2003 the bipedal *Ardipithecus kadabba* (5.6 million years old) was found, which might be an even earlier ancestor according to some scientists.

Manmade stone tools found in both Afar and the Omo Valley date to between 2.5–2.6 million years old. Early hominids are assumed to have migrated northward and eastward initially, and to have established other populations from which modern racial groupings have been formed. Perhaps the name given by Ethiopians for the Blue Nile—Ghion, also used in the Book of Genesis for one of the four rivers of Eden—reflects this earliest of early times?

Ethiopia's antiquity is seen in numerous rock paintings throughout the country, some up to 10,000 years old. Although harder to date, Ethiopia is also known to be a major center of early plant domestication and crop diversity: the staple grain, *teff*, as well as the oilseed *nug*, finger millet, *chat*, and coffee, whether imported or native, have sufficient unique variations to indicate a very long history of cultivated farming in the area.

In the annals of documented history from Egypt, mention is made of goods being sent from an area of Ethiopia to the Pharaohs, in about 3500 BCE. This area in the southern Red Sea, known as the Land of Punt, rich in myrrh, gold, ivory, and slaves, might be in Tigray or in the Somali region. The Greek Ptolemaic rulers of Egypt from the early fourth century BCE specifically mention the port of Adulis in their writings, which is very close to present-day Massawa in Eritrea. The Greeks also gave Ethiopia, which means "the Land of Burned Faces," its name.

Signs of the first civilization in the area appeared halfway through the first millennium BCE. The stone palaces and buildings at Yeha, twenty miles (32 kilometers) east of Axum, along with numerous other sites, reveal a rich culture very similar in religion, language, and architecture to that of Saba, southern Arabia.

By 100 CE the Kingdom of Axum was born—a rich trading nation with a foot on both sides of the Red Sea, routes to Egypt both inland and by the Red Sea, and trails to the south, where valuable commodities could be obtained. The Axumites spoke a Semitic language similar to the liturgical language of Ge'ez, which they originally wrote in a Sabaean script; they worshiped many gods with Sabaean names and they also identified with Greek gods; and they minted coins. They built impressive stone palaces, and erected tall

Axumite coins from the 5th century CE.

stone *stelae* (pillars, or vertical obelisks)—one of them, at 520 tons and 108 feet (33 meters) high, is the largest stone object known to have been worked by stone cutters.

Modern Beginnings in Axum

Modern Ethiopia is based on this Kingdom of Axum, which, under King Ezana, embraced the Christian Gospel in about 330 CE. On Ezana's coins, and in inscriptions around town, the Christian cross replaced pagan symbols. In this way, Ezana determined not only Ethiopia's dominant religion today, but also the region's dominant Semitic languages, its literacy, and its continued links with the eastern Mediterranean. Despite the Kingdom of Axum's decline in the eighth century, when the rise of Islamic trade isolated Ethiopia, the hallmarks of the period remain to this day.

The Rise of a Feudal Nation: the Medieval Period
Ethiopia emerged from undocumented obscurity early in the second millennium as an advanced monarchical nation. Its empire and kingdoms, sometimes based in Tigray, sometimes farther west or south, in Shoa, waxed and waned during the subsequent centuries largely unnoticed by Western Europe. The feudal model was a means of organizing the country and providing soldiers for war, and was centered on an elaborate and sophisticated royal court. Western Europeans only became conscious of Ethiopia during the Crusades, when it was seen as an ally against the Muslims. The legend of Prester John, the ruler of a Christian kingdom surrounded by Muslims, arose in Europe in the mid-twelfth century.

From Axum, power shifted south to Lasta, where the monarchs of the Zagwe Dynasty, c.900–1270 CE, established their rule. They left no literature and their greatest achievement was the creation of the Lalibela rock churches, built to represent Jerusalem. Later emperors ruled as descendants of King Solomon of Israel, their claim justified in an illustrated document known as the *Kebra Negast,* (*Book of the Glory of Kings*) written in the fourteenth century. It tells the Ethiopian version of the story of the Queen of Sheba's visit to Jerusalem to witness Solomon's riches as told in the biblical Book of Kings. The *Kebra Negast* continues the story with a tale of Solomon's fathering of a child by the Queen of Sheba. This child was Ethiopia's apocryphal first emperor, Menelik I. He was said to have taken the Ark of the Covenant, which housed the stone tablets given by God to Moses, and kept in Solomon's temple in Jerusalem, down the Nile for safekeeping in Ethiopia. Today, these tablets are closely guarded in the Church of St. Mary of Zion in Axum, and their authenticity is impossible to verify.

This was a Christian society, with strong Judaic elements, in which scholars flourished and literacy was nurtured in monasteries. Pilgrimage to Jerusalem increased contact with Europeans. A diplomatic mission of thirty men was sent from Ethiopia to Spain and Rome in the early fourteenth century, and later, in the 1390s, a Florentine trader appeared in Ethiopia. Martial skills had high value as aristocrats all over the country, jostling for influence at court, were expected to support the emperor's wars. The series of dynasties that ruled during these centuries owed their survival, or not, to leaders with extraordinary political skill and military prowess.

Defending Ethiopia's Christian Heritage

By the sixteenth century Ethiopia's trading rivalry with its Muslim neighbors was the torch that nearly led to

defeat for the Christian descendants of Axum.
The most successful Muslim commander was
Mohammed Gragn ("the Left-Handed"), from the
Emirate of Adal in the lowlands. He had access to
superior arms from the Ottomans, and waged a *jihad*
("holy war"), defeating Emperor Lebna Dengel in
1529, and continuing to overrun most of eastern and
southern Ethiopia. Christian Ethiopia was saved by
the assistance of the Portuguese, known to the
Ethiopians from an earlier diplomatic mission,
who were the Ottomans' main rivals on the East
African coast. Mohammed Gragn was finally
defeated in 1541.

At the same time, a migration of Cushitic-
speaking and pagan Oromo clans was moving
northward to settle widely in the highlands. They
added another dimension to Ethiopia's political and
demographic mix, and have entirely changed the
ethnic makeup of southern and western Ethiopia.

In 1557, Jesuit missionaries from Portugal
arrived. They set up missions with ornate churches
and buildings, still seen near Lake Tana, but were
summarily expelled by Emperor Fasilidas in 1632,
following a miscalculated conversion to Catholicism
by his predecessor. Foreigners were then barred
from entering the country. From the beginning of
the eighteenth century until the rise of Emperor
Tewodros, there followed, in biblical terminology,
a chaotic "Time of the Judges" (*mesafent*),
characterized by infighting, which weakened the
central authority of the emperors.

The Nineteenth Century and the Beginnings of Modernization

A semblance of order arrived with a brilliant warlord from the west, who was crowned Emperor Tewodros in 1855. He offered a sense of national unity and marked out a process of military, land, and Church reform. The Emperor built up a good rapport with certain foreigners, but, tragically, he suffered from bipolar disorder and paranoia and eventually took his own life at Maqdala, in 1868, when a British military expedition was sent to rescue a number of foreigners held hostage by him on a mountaintop.

By now Ethiopia was being drawn into international affairs by the march of European and Ottoman imperialism, and by its own need for guns and other supplies. Tewodros' successor, the Tigrayan Yohannes IV, was killed by Sudanese Mahdists at Galabat in 1889. This gave a Shoan king from the south the opportunity to seize his chance. He was crowned Emperor Menelik II (the first Menelik had been the son of Solomon of Israel). His first major confrontation was with the Italians, then in control of present-day Eritrea and keen to expand into Ethiopia. At the Battle of Adwa in 1896, Menelik's victory against the better armed, but numerically inferior, European force had a palpable effect on both sides. Menelik then turned his attention to expansion, pushing the limits of his authority southward, westward, and eastward, until he came up against the territorial ambitions of the French and the British colonial powers then in present-day Djibouti, Somalia, and Kenya.

His empire secured, Menelik II now devoted time to modernization. A new capital, Addis Ababa, was established on the southernmost edge of Christian Ethiopia, now the center of the country. Like rulers before and after him, Menelik took care in choosing

Emperor Menelik II.

European advisers, trying not to be too reliant on any one nation. He was devoted in particular to his Swiss adviser, Alfred Ilg, but he also used the French to build a railway, the Russians to build the first hospital, the Italians the first road in Addis Ababa, and the British a bank.

Emperor Haile Selassie, Ethiopia's Last Monarch

Haile Selassie's rise to power in the early twentieth century was, like that of his predecessors, paved with blood. After Menelik II's death in 1913, his grandson, Iyasu, ruled uncertainly before being deposed in 1916. Menelik's daughter, Zauditu, was then proclaimed Empress, though real power lay with a cousin, Ras Teferi, who was made Regent. He had won a battle against Iyasu's father, Mikael, at Sagale in 1916, thereby gaining the foothold he needed. He was intelligent, able, and familiar with the outside world, having been educated by a French priest in Harar. He was eventually crowned Emperor Haile Selassie in 1930.

Ras Teferi instigated another burst of progressive projects, again with the help of a medley of foreign advisers. He employed White Russians to train his army, he outlawed slavery, and, in 1923, took Ethiopia into the League of Nations. Progress was halted when the Italians, avenging Adwa, mounted a brutal campaign in late 1935 to occupy Ethiopia, and the Emperor went into exile in Britain. However, the Italians never managed to overcome resistance in the countryside and fully colonize Ethiopia as they had intended.

Following Italy's entry into the Second World War, a combination of British Commonwealth and Ethiopian Patriot forces attacked the Italians from all sides in 1941. Emperor Haile Selassie made a triumphal re-entry to his capital on May 5, the day he had left it five years earlier. He then had to reestablish his authority. Tragically, most of the Western-educated elite had either been murdered or had gone into exile, making it more difficult to resume the process

Haile Selassie, Emperor of Ethiopia from 1930–1974.

of modernization. But in time he gave the country a new constitution and re-wrote the criminal and civil codes. In his foreign relations he became closer to the USA and other Western nations. During the Cold War he sent troops with the UN to the Korean War and to the Congo. In the 1960s Haile Selassie supported the decolonization movement in Africa, and enabled Nelson Mandela to have military training in Ethiopia. He was instrumental in the formation of the Organization of African Unity (now the African Union) and established its headquarters in Addis Ababa in 1963.

To the north, in Eritrea, however, Haile Selassie sowed the seeds of future trouble. After Italy lost the war in 1941, a British military government administered the territory until 1952, when a decision was made by the UN to take the territory into federation with Ethiopia. In 1962 Haile Selassie dissolved Eritrea's parliament and formally annexed Eritrea as Ethiopia's fourteenth province in order to control an independence movement that had emerged to shake off Ethiopian rule.

Increasingly, Haile Selassie failed to balance traditional forces with the new intelligentsia who had links with the Communist world. Following an attempted coup in 1960, an expensive war with Somalia over the Ogaden region in 1964, and a famine in 1972, he was deposed by radical elements in the armed forces in 1974.

Marxist Rule (1974–91)

After Haile Selassie's overthrow, Mengistu Haile Mariam emerged as leader of the Marxist Provisional Military Administrative Council, known as the Derg. He ruled for fourteen years until he himself was deposed in 1991. Opposition to the Derg was immediate. The intelligentsia took to the streets and, in the Derg's crackdown known as the Red Terror, many thousands of people died. Yet again, educated Ethiopians were either eliminated or went into exile.

Opposition to Derg rule also grew within the provinces: the Eritreans, as well as the Oromo, Tigrayans, and Somalis in Ogaden, all took their cue and mounted secessionist campaigns. Dissatisfaction with the central government was stoked by the Derg's stranglehold on the economy and the resultant shortage of food, by an unpopular resettlement program, and by a disastrous drought in Wollo and Tigray in 1984–85. After years of civil war, the end came in May 1991 when Meles Zenawi's tanks, supported by the Eritrean forces and backed by the USA, rumbled into Addis Ababa, instigating a radical new direction for the country.

The two generally recognized contributions to Ethiopia's development made by the Derg, with its socialist ideals, were to extend primary schooling for children and to release the peasantry from their subservience to landowners. For the first time the peasants had a voice through the *kebele* (local council) system that had been set up throughout the country, and that still exists today.

Meles Zenawi and Ethnic Federalism (1991–2012)

Meles Zenawi, who had headed up the Tigrayan liberation movement, became leader of the Ethiopian People's Revolutionary Democratic Front (EPRDF) coalition from 1991 until his death in 2012. The EPRDF was made up of parties from around the country that combined to overthrow the Derg government.

Meles's most significant policy was to revise Ethiopian provincial boundaries into ethno-linguistic regions; while, externally, Eritrea finally gained its

independence from
Ethiopia in 1993 after
a referendum. The
consequences of
both events remain
potent today.

Meles Zanawi, 2012.

The leaders of both
countries came from very
similar Orthodox Christian
and Tigrinya-speaking
backgrounds, with parents
from both countries,
and initially cooperated
well together. However,
the differences between Meles and his counterpart,
Isaias Afewerki, soon deepened. In 1998, war broke
out over a disputed boundary in a poorly populated
and infertile piece of land. Bitter trench warfare was
conducted for two years, thousands of lives were lost
on both sides, and both treasuries were drained to pay
for arms. A peace accord was achieved in 2000, but
the borders remained closed.

Ethnic federalism remains a contentious solution
to ruling Ethiopia's many parts. Under Meles, who
had personal authority and a strong approach to law
and order, tensions were kept in check. However, this
led to increased assertiveness in some of Ethiopia's
regions, which has been difficult for Meles's two
successors to manage.

Meles also came to power as an economic reformer.
He pushed for agriculture-led development, which had

its successes. The economy grew fast, and a frenzy of rural road building, and dams for hydroelectricity, bear testimony to his vision.

Meles's unexpected death in 2012 brought another EPRDF coalition partner, Hailemariam Desalegn, into power. He had to deal with increasingly unsettled regions, particularly in Oromia, where disturbances fueled by diaspora Ethiopians often had fatal results. Hailemariam voluntarily resigned in 2018, making way for the appointment of another EPRDF member, Dr. Abiy Ahmed.

Abiy Ahmed—mediator and reconciler (2018–)

A protestant Christian who represents an Oromo constituency near Jimma, Ahmed won a Nobel Peace Prize in October 2019, a mere 18 months after taking office. His success on the international stage is generally admired; his standing inside Ethiopia is more ambiguous.

When he became leader, Ahmed immediately set about trying to settle the border dispute with Eritrea by agreeing to give up territory. His success met with jubilant response among thousands of families on both sides of the border, although the issue has proved intractable and the border closed once again. In 2019 Ahmed brokered another peace deal in Sudan, when the interim military government of Sudan agreed to step down in favor of civilian rule.

Opposition within Ethiopia was also tackled in the same non-confrontational way. Ahmed lifted a state of emergency, ordered the release of prisoners, allowed exiled dissidents to return home, and unblocked websites and TV channels, which greatly lightened the atmosphere and allowed people to speak and write more freely. In December 2019, a new party, called the Ethiopian Prosperity Party, was formed out of all but one of the constituent parties of the EPRDF.

By this point, ethnic federalism, designed to provide equal justice to Ethiopia's parts, had penetrated national life too deeply to avoid divisiveness at the start of Ahmed's rule. In November 2019, the Sidama people, a constituent part of the SNNP Region, voted to form their own semi-autonomous regional state. Others may follow. Violent demonstrations in Oromia in 2019 shocked Ethiopia's people into a new determination to find an Ethiopian identity that relies less on ethnicity, and more on shared history.

GOVERNMENT AND POLITICS

The art of governing Ethiopia has always been to balance centralized authority with regional devolution. It has never been easy to unify the country and please all its parts.

The new constitution of 1995 gave parliament two chambers: the larger is the Council of People's Representatives, with 547 constituency members elected for five-year terms; and the Council of the Federation, which has 110 members drawn from the regions. The president is elected, by a joint session of both houses of parliament, for six years, and the prime minister is elected by a majority in the House of People's Representatives.

For administrative purposes the country is divided into the ten ethnically based regions and two chartered cities. At the local level the regions are divided hierarchically into zones, *woredas*, and *kebeles* (local community councils).

The judiciary is officially independent, and administered by the Ministry of Justice. Legal jurisdiction is shared between the federal government and the Regional States. The president of the Federal Supreme Court is recommended by the prime minister and appointed by the House of People's Representatives. The Civil, Criminal and Commercial codes, based on the Napoleonic Code, were introduced under Emperor Haile Selassie, and incorporates aspects of traditional Ethiopian law. Liberal values, such as human rights and independence of the judiciary, are enshrined in the Constitution. Contract law, property law, company and trade law also reflect Western values. Other aspects of the constitution, such as the recognition of nations and peoples as subjects of certain rights, including the right to secede, and the public ownership of land are uniquely Ethiopian. While the legal system is well developed, the judiciary is seen by many to be inexperienced and lacking in training.

THE ECONOMY

The Ethiopian economy is mainly based on peasant agriculture. It is challenged by high population growth and a shortage of foreign exchange. The Marxist model of the Derg years has been replaced with one known as the "Developmental State," in which the government keeps control of key infrastructures, such as the airlines and telecommunications, while liberalizing other sectors of the economy. Beginning with agriculture-led developments such as rural road building, irrigation, and investment in energy to provide better infrastructure for smallholders, a series of Growth and Transformation Plans (GTPs) are leading the economy toward greater diversity and industrialization.

Private investment has been partially liberalized, and there is now more commercial farming, particularly in horticulture and coffee growing. A vast expansion of regional universities and technical colleges match the building of business and industrial parks around major towns. Investment from China and Turkey in pharmaceuticals, leather, and textile industries has fueled much of this growth. Tourism is also a growing sector.

The growth rate of the economy during the last twenty years has impressed observers, and poverty levels have fallen from 55 percent down to 30 percent of the population. The economy, however, is still principally reliant on peasant farming and there has been no progress on reversing the balance of payments deficit. The principle of state ownership of some utilities is being eroded as the government seeks to open up these sectors to private investors who would bring in necessary foreign exchange. The critical shortage of foreign exchange also makes it difficult to pay for improving the infrastructure.

Climate change is expected to have a severe impact on agriculture, something GTPs have tried to address, with emphasis placed on climate resilience.

All agricultural land was nationalized in 1975 and remains so, but farmers have usufruct rights, which means they are able to use and benefit from the property of others. Foreigners and local investors can lease land for periods of up to forty years, depending on the region. Some investors have met with difficulties in enforcing a lease contract. Agricultural products provide approximately 40 percent of GDP and 80 percent of exports, in the form of coffee, *chat*, cattle, grains, hides, oilseeds, pulses, cotton, sugarcane, cut flowers, sheep, goats, and fish.

The Ethiopian Commodities Exchange (ECX) for coffee, sesame seeds, haricot beans, maize, and wheat was inaugurated in 2008, though specialty coffee is allowed to bypass the ECX. There is no stock exchange as yet.

Ethiopia has the potential to produce 30,000 megawatts of electricity (enough for the country's needs and for export), from hydroelectric schemes on the Abay (Blue Nile), the Tekezze, Omo, and the Awash rivers, and also through geothermal plants. Infrastructure to provide electricity to small villages, however, is underdeveloped and most people rely on burning eucalyptus wood for their cooking needs. All fuel oil is imported via Sudan and Djibouti.

Gold is the most valuable mineral mined in Ethiopia, although there are large reserves of lower value minerals for construction that are of high quality. There is a significant inflow of hard currency from remittances by expatriate Ethiopians in America and Europe.

INTERNATIONAL RELATIONS

Ethiopians have always tried to balance foreign influences to their advantage. For example, they maintain close relations with Israel as well as with Arab countries, and with China and Russia, as well as with the USA and the European Union. Addis Ababa is the diplomatic center of Africa, with the headquarters of the African Union in the city, and every African country maintaining a diplomatic mission there. The United Nations' Economic Commission for Africa (ECA) is housed in the historic Africa Hall, off Meskel Square.

Ethiopia shares concerns about radical Islam with other neighboring countries in the region. Its forces are engaged in maintaining peace in Somalia and in South Sudan. Although relations with Eritrea were broken during the Ethio–Eritrean border war 1998–2000, these are being repaired. Ethiopia supports the official, though contested, government of neighboring Somalia; and also maintains close relations with the internationally unrecognized Republic of Somaliland (a former British colony); with Djibouti; and with Sudan and South Sudan. The headwaters of the Nile are a topic for perennial discussion in Ethiopia's relations with Egypt.

CHAPTER TWO

VALUES & ATTITUDES

NATIONAL IDENTITY

Modern Ethiopia is the product of a long history, an ancient kingdom, peopled by a mixture of ethnicities, living in, and below, high mountain plateaus in the Horn of Africa. Once an empire, today it is a federation of nations with a distinctive common culture that embraces and holds together several greater and lesser regional subcultures.

Since their conversion to Christianity in the fourth century, highland Ethiopians have shared a tradition of law and moral philosophy based on books written in Ge'ez, their ancient common language, with its unique script, still used in churches today.

When the empire expanded to the south, west, and east of its historic core in the nineteenth century, it brought into the Ethiopian fold Muslim and pagan peoples, with Protestant and Catholic Christianity also added to the mix. Rapid modernization in the twentieth century, with its attendant Western democratic values, contributed to an already rich culture.

> ### Red in Tooth and Claw
>
> "The eye of the leopard is on the goat, and the eye of the goat is on the leaf."
>
> Ethiopian proverb

So what is *Ityopyawinet*, the Amharic word for the distinct quality of being Ethiopian? Ethiopians find it easy to recognize and hard to define. For many it is about being part of a rich mix of cultures in which the virtues of humility, politeness, and patience are practiced. For others it is more about their shared history, rather than their shared differences. At best, their awareness of the strengths and weaknesses of each contributing part of their culture enables them to cooperate in a spirit of nationhood. That said, Ethiopians can be extraordinarily competitive between themselves. Although they are fiercely proud of their own cultural mix and are hospitable to guests and strangers, they can appear secretive and treat foreigners or other races with disdain. Ethiopians value deep relationships, yet have difficulty sustaining them. They can be cheerful and generous, while having a deeply pessimistic view of human nature. Ethiopians are seldom surprised by betrayal, and can maintain personal feuds for decades. They are often individualistic rather than team players, methodical rather than intuitive, intellectual rather than creative. In short, they understand well the subtlety of paradox, but struggle with contradiction.

ETHIOPIA'S CULTURES

Amhara
The masterful Amhara possess great political acumen and protect their corner with patience and skill. They are the traditional ruling class, and the speakers of Ethiopia's centuries-old national language, Amharic, which has its own script, and is susceptible of ambiguity to a remarkable degree. They can at times be proud and impulsive.

> #### What's in a Name?
> Amhara personal names are often expressive of aspirations to mastery: *Asselefech* ("she made them line up"), *Asfa Wossen* ("expand the borders"), *Mulugeta* ("master of all"), and, indeed, *Muluimabet* "mistress of all."

Amharas have a tradition of writing clever, short poems, with an overt meaning and a hidden meaning, referred to as "wax and gold."

Gurage
Gurage people, from the highlands on the western scarp of the Rift Valley, are traders and know the value of

money. They are not easily cheated, and dominate much of Addis Ababa's shopkeeping. They also dominate the vegetable growing sector. The Ethiopian banana tree, called *enset*, is used by the Gurage as their principal food source, while the tree's fronds and fibers have many important everyday and ritual-related uses. Guragues speak a Semitic language, and trace their origins to Gura, a district now in Eritrea.

Oromo

The Oromo people, with diverse clans, though speaking one language, often more easily identify with sub-units; they are difficult to generalize about. Widely considered hardworking, loyal, and fun-loving, they have a well-known affinity with the natural world and are admired for their horsemanship. They now form Ethiopia's largest nation and pride themselves on a system of egalitarian ethics known as *gada*, and on their tradition of consensus. A more pronounced sense of nationhood has risen of late, and their language, with its many dialects, has recently enjoyed a renaissance and is now used throughout the state of Oromia.

Tigray

Tigrayans see their land as the cradle of Ethiopian Christianity and civilization, and tend to give their children names that reflect this; "Servant of Mary" (*Gabre Mariam*), and "Power of the Trinity" (*Haile Selassie*). Tigrayans historically have survived by skillful management of their relations with the other Ethiopian peoples. Their language is the closest descendant of

A Tigray farmer.

ancient Ge'ez, and carries over the border into highland
Eritrea. Their territory includes Axum, the oldest city
in Ethiopia and its ecclesiastical capital. There are
numerous pre-Axumite archaeological sites in Tigray,
including Bet Samati and Yeha.

Other Peoples

Added to the contemporary mix are Somalis, Afars,
and Aderes, who have a Muslim tradition of
government by sultans, or chiefs. Gambella and Beni
Shangul peoples of the west, the Sidamo and Welayta
peoples of the south, and the other smaller nations
of the south have an animistic tradition but are now
embracing protestant Christianity.

A Karo woman in Omo Valley, south Ethiopia.

ATTITUDES TOWARD FOREIGNERS

White foreigners are commonly, and usually affectionately, called *ferenj*, an Arabic word meaning "Frankish." Ethiopians will often form genuine friendships with *ferenj*, although the latter will find the maintenance of these relationships demand loyalty and face to face contact. Asians, other Africans, and Arabs, along with Greeks, Italians, and Armenians who have married Ethiopians, or who are of mixed race and speak fluent Amharic, are scarcely treated as foreigners at all. Ethiopians, while enjoying the company of foreigners, can also be wary of their intent. In some areas, *ferenj* can be subject to mocking curiosity. This is changing for the better. The increasing number of Ethiopians living in North America and Europe makes it more likely foreigners will be treated with understanding.

There is less subtlety toward short-term foreigners, diplomats, and tourists, who are often regarded as fair game to be exploited. Big hotels are notorious for hustlers, people who attach themselves ruthlessly to foreigners at the gate, refusing to let them go until they have obtained some favor from them.

ATTITUDES TOWARD BORDERS AND NEIGHBORS

Ethiopia's borders have been, for the most part, permeable and sometimes undemarcated. To the east, Somalis from the states of Djibouti, Somaliland, and Somalia interact constantly with the Somali region of Ethiopia, whose inhabitants form 6 percent of the Ethiopian population. Somalis are represented in the Ethiopian government and there are many thousands of Somalis resident in Addis Ababa.

In the same way, the Nuer and Anuak peoples of Southern Sudan, who also form the core population of the Gambella region of Ethiopia, are found in large numbers in Addis Ababa, and are recognized as citizens of Ethiopia.

Kenya to the south is thought of as a friendly neighboring state, and although Borana and Somali people, who are common to both countries, straddle the border, it is recognized that the Kenyan heartland is a different country.

Ethiopia's relationship with Eritrea to the north is in the nature of sibling rivalry: Eritrea can be both the closest and the most hostile of Ethiopia's neighbors. A costly war was fought between the countries from 1998–2000. Once part of Ethiopia's borderlands, colonized by Italy, and then unhappily "reunited with the motherland" from 1951–1991, Eritrea shares a culture, a Christian Church, a cuisine, and a common language with Tigray in Ethiopia. Many Eritreans continue to live in Ethiopia and are well integrated into Ethiopian life.

RELIGIOUS TRADITION AND MODERN ASPIRATION

There has always been a tension in Ethiopian culture between conservative religious values and the aspiration to be *zemenawi*, or "modern." Many people are very devout, and the rest are tolerant and respectful of religion. Both the Orthodox and Muslim faiths have formed the Ethiopian character, which is patient, fatalistic, and long-suffering. Nevertheless, the long-standing and deep-seated belief in modernization, particularly by its rulers, is coupled with the faint suspicion that churches and mosques have been obstacles in the path of this.

Ethiopians often long to live abroad, to get an education there and better their material circumstances. During the monarchy, young intellectuals went abroad and returned home resolved to be begetters of change and agents of modernization. Nowadays, many seek to join relatives in settling permanently in the main cities of the Western world, particularly in North America, where they form distinct communities.

This new diaspora is itself influential in the homeland in many ways, both as an object of envy and admiration to those who have stayed back home, and as a major source of remittance income, which, among other things, also supports opposition politicians. Back in Ethiopia, increasing Westernization has seen a more confident materialism take hold, and a rapid growth in Protestant Christianity.

EDUCATION

Ethiopians have always set a high value on education. Once the preserve of the Orthodox Church, literacy is common across the country. Indeed, one of the generally recognized successes of the Derg government was to substantially improve the literacy level of the population. Traditionally, education and the ability to speak, read, and write Amharic, led to a secure place in government service and a status in society. Higher education continues to provide the means to an influential job, with students aspiring to become doctors, airline pilots, and engineers. Accordingly, the state is providing schools, colleges, and universities in all the major towns. The language of education, however, has altered. From an early age, children are taught English, and take other

lessons in their vernacular language. Amharic is
no longer as widely known as it was. Despite state
provision, families will make huge sacrifices to provide
a private education for their children, to spare them the
overcrowded "shift system," and give them an edge in
the English language. Many graduates today still find
their way into government service.

HIERARCHY AND ADMINISTRATION

Northern Ethiopians in particular are deeply conscious
of hierarchy, a system with centuries of refinement.
Government offices of all kinds throughout the land,
and in the remotest outposts, will house a group

of very competent and efficient bureaucrats, often operating out of meager buildings. These offices are subject to frequent reorganization, but are always run hierarchically, with the big person at the top seated behind a large desk, and a table placed lengthwise in front of it with six to eight chairs along each side. He or she may be protected by a secretary, who controls entry to the big person's office—but there is a general presumption that anybody has access to these offices, and to the people at the top.

The administration, likewise, is organized hierarchically, with the country divided into regions, the regions divided into zones, the zones divided into *woredas*, and the *woredas* divided into *kebeles*. Officials will enforce policies at appropriate levels; requests will be passed up the hierarchy, and orders will be passed down.

MILITARISM

Militarism is a traditional virtue and carries respect in Ethiopia. Power has almost always been gained militarily, and the military itself seen as an effective arm of government; many Ethiopians see the use of force to control dissenters and disaffected groups as a necessity. With a natural tendency to hierarchy, and a need to place oneself under the protection of a powerful patron, the obligation to bear and use arms was always unquestioned in the feudal era. Nowadays, there is a professional standing army and air force. There is no national service and no conscription, but the armed forces are adequately manned, and pacifism is unheard of. Readiness to fight to protect the country's freedoms, and its national territory, remains part of Ethiopia's national psyche.

DEMOCRACY AND HUMAN RIGHTS

Ethiopia is nearer to being a democracy today than ever before in its history, but it is a country in transition— from a deeply autocratic monarchy, through communist dictatorship, to a federal parliamentary republic with a ceremonial head of state. Elections are held regularly, but there is ambiguity about the commitment of government to real choice. It is instructive, when searching for clues as to where real decision making takes place, to look beyond the usual instruments of democracy, such as parliament and the judicial system, and be aware that much happens behind the scenes. This political approach is entrenched in Ethiopia, where so many are economically insecure, making a connection between one's job, and links with a ruling party, especially pertinent.

The Power of Patronage

"Whatever shines is the Sun, and whoever rules is our King."

Tigrinya proverb

Parliament, and the city and regional assemblies, do meet nonetheless, government is criticized, and the authorities are occasionally satirized openly. Newspapers express a variety of political views.

Prime Minister Ahmed may well have released many dissenters from prison, yet individual human rights have traditionally not figured highly on the national agenda. On the other hand, it is noticeable that humor and caricature flourish as a form of political critique when the atmosphere lightens. The question being debated presently is what kind of democracy does Ethiopia need: ethnic federalism or unitary government, or a system in between?

It is worth mentioning that the involvement of foreigners in political or human rights cases or causes is not tolerated. If you do choose to get involved, you will probably be expelled from the country. A law was passed in January 2009 preventing foreign charities, or local charities funded from abroad, from engaging in such activities.

ATTITUDES TO THE ENVIRONMENT

The natural world is valued in principle and many parks and preserves exist, including the oldest conserved forest in Africa, Menagasha-Suba near Addis Ababa, planted by Emperor Zara Yakob in the fifteenth century. But a burgeoning population of both people and cattle tends to undermine the best conservation efforts.

In the past, land degradation was most acute in the
north where marauding armies fought for dominance
and farm workers were conscripted. Religious
sensibilities, however, helped to preserve copses of
trees within the compounds of Orthodox churches
after other woodland was cut; and the Oromo people's
regard for the *oda,* or wild fig tree, has provided
beautiful scatterings of these giant trees in arable
fields of the south.

Ethiopia has struggled to maintain the integrity
of some of its conservation parks as people need to
make a livelihood. Individual families make inroads
into unprotected as well as protected forest, often on
mountainsides. In the lowlands, where cows are viewed
as wealth, herds are found grazing in parks, as well as
causing degradation outside them.

There is, however, widespread publicity to educate
people about care for future resources, and the
preservation of unique flora and fauna finds approval
among a people proud of the distinctive nature of their
wildlife. Led from the top, there are public tree planting
days, communal terracing of slopes, and policies
dealing with the detritus of modern life, such as vehicle
pollution and plastic.

Ethiopians have a strong sense of natural beauty.
City dwellers offer flowers as gifts, and upgrade their
cities with trees, while countryside people will decorate
the floors of their houses with flowers and grass.

Orthodox Christians in Ethiopia have adopted
certain Old Testament taboos against eating animals
such as wild duck, antelope, pigs, and camels.

Domestic animals, such as dogs, donkeys, and horses, are often treated as functionaries, and poverty will often prevent them from being fed properly or seen by a vet. However, Ethiopians can be sentimental and reluctant to kill an animal to put it out of its misery.

ATTITUDES TO PAIN AND SUFFERING

The approach to pain and suffering is one of stoicism and fatalism. If God will not remove it, you need to bear it.

There are evidently many poor people in Ethiopia. Their condition is more extreme in the cities where family ties may be lacking. Traditionally, begging outside church gates provided a form of social security—begging is in no way shameful. Indeed, supplication is done throughout all levels of society, but it is combined with an extraordinary patient endurance of hardship and pain.

Sick people often do not consult a doctor unless the symptoms are very advanced. Both modern medicine and traditional medicine are used, along with holy water from a saint's shrine as an extra precaution.

Families are expected to support their members, and anyone from a large poor family who "makes good" is expected to support his or her relatives for many years. Because of this, eating in public is avoided unless the food is shared. In Ethiopian cities, rich and poor live in the same neighborhoods, and the incongruity of having slums nestling next to opulent hotels elicits little comment from Ethiopians.

There has always been a wealthy class in Ethiopia, so poor people are used to discreet displays of wealth. Among the rich, wealth was often not flaunted and was despised on ascetic grounds, unless at a wedding. However, as mentioned, today there is a growing materialism and more ostentation as a result of Western influences. Nowadays, many of those in the middle class will aspire to live in gated compounds to maintain their privacy.

ATTITUDES TO DEATH

When an Ethiopian dies, close mourners will beat their breasts and cry openly, while others maintain a respectful silence. The funeral follows very quickly, as is the case in hot countries, and is always a burial, not a cremation (see pages 85–86). The bodies of people who die overseas are often flown home for burial. During the burial procession Ethiopians, if driving past, will slow down and bow respectfully toward the deceased's coffin. Foreigners who drive past carelessly are considered insensitive.

In the mourning tent erected near the deceased's home, callers will sit, normally in silence or quiet conversation. Wealthy Christian Ethiopians will have a large memorial stone, or mausoleum, while Muslims will erect a more modest stone pillar.

GENDER AND SEXUALITY

Women are not as subservient in Ethiopia as in some parts of the Middle East. In the early twentieth century Ethiopia had a female reigning empress, and a powerful Queen consort. Today, women are prominent in business, law, administration, and politics. Nevertheless, women are expected to cook and serve food for men, and commonly do this with easy grace.

In the countryside it is different. Women fetch water, and carry a large share of the tasks of rural life. Girls are sometimes married very young in the countryside, increasing the risks of death or injury in childbirth. The practice of female circumcision, or female genital mutilation, remains widespread, but is not universal. The operation, designed to diminish sexual pleasure for women, is found among both Muslim and Christian communities.

Although women are expected to be virgins until marriage, Ethiopian attitudes to sex are not puritanical. Heterosexual prostitution is not particularly shameful. However, gay sex is universally frowned upon. It is illegal for men, and assumed unthinkable for women. This does not mean that there is no homosexuality in Ethiopia, but it does mean that it is very much undercover, and seldom acknowledged. The Amharic for male gay sex is *gebre sodom*—sodomy.

The sexual abuse of young people by foreigners attracts severe penalties.

WORK ETHIC AND ATTITUDES TO TIME

Ethiopians are generally good at systematic, cerebral work. They have fine lawyers, accountants, airplane pilots, surgeons, and engineers, professions that demand systematic mental skills—and they provide respected visionary statesmen on the world stage. On the other hand, middle managers are often unwilling to take responsibility or to make decisions for fear of losing their job.

White-collar jobs, based at a desk, are more highly valued than those involving practical activity, trade, or manufacturing. People are often happier in a situation where they have carefully defined responsibilities, less content to be in a situation where there are no boundaries.

Written commitments are almost never broken. Verbal agreements are not as binding and for this reason are often preferred. Official letters from a company or an organization should always carry a seal, or ink stamps, as well as a signature.

Cash is the preferred method of payment, though card payments are increasingly common. Transactions should always be made against a receipt, and large sums should be paid in front of witnesses. Checks are also still used.

Ethiopians can generally be relied upon to be on time for appointments, although they refer self-deprecatingly to an *abasha ketero* ("Abyssinian appointment"), when they fear they may be late. It is recognized that it is not always easy to be on time in the face of Addis Ababa's sometimes horrendous traffic jams, and unpunctuality may be forgiven.

Foreign visitors are often surprised by a business phone call shortly after 7:00 a.m. Although normal working hours begin at 8:30 a.m., people are on the road early, and cell phones have made it easier to set up all the day's appointments before breakfast.

People do not generally phone each other after 9:30 p.m., and dinner parties usually end at about that time.

In the countryside, timekeeping is not given such high value. People observe the cycles of the agricultural year and work hard as families or communities. Small children learn from an early age the importance of tending animals and helping in the harvest. Their daily routine is defined by the weekly or twice weekly markets, by the seasons, and by time off for the traditional communal activities such as attending church or celebrating a wedding.

In town or country, you will encounter an early rising, meticulous, and methodical people who will work hard to put food on the table for their own advancement.

CHAPTER THREE

RELIGION & TRADITION

Many Ethiopians are deeply religious; others are respectful of religion. Orthodox Christian faith and practice is in a tradition unique to Ethiopia, with more than 40 percent of the population belonging to the Ethiopian Orthodox Church. About a third of Ethiopians are Sunni Muslims, mainly to the east and southeast of the country. A fifth of the populations belong to other Christian denominations, and there are animists, mostly among tribes to the south and west.

Ethiopia's tiny Jewish community has almost all emigrated, mostly to Israel. Immigrant West Indian Rastafarians, who follow the cult of Emperor Haile Selassie, are said to be increasing.

ORTHODOX CHRISTIANITY

Orthodoxy, as practiced in Ethiopia, is an ancient form of Christianity. It teaches reliance on saintly intercessors,

The church of Saint George in Lalibela, a holy city and a place of pilgrimage in an area known for its rock-hewn churches.

and its canon of scripture includes apocryphal books of the Bible, such as Enoch and Jubilees. Orthodoxy is not, however, a static Church, and in the twentieth century it has embraced changes such as the use of the vernacular language in preaching and in worship.

Saints of the Orthodox Church appear everywhere: in paintings inside churches, in iconic representations sold on the street, and at sacred places associated with them. Mary, mother of Christ, is the most revered; Gebre Menfes Kiddus (known as *Abo*), associated with Mt. Zukwala, near Debre Zeit, is the "St. Francis" of Ethiopia, shown surrounded by animals; St. Tekle Haimanot is a historical figure from the thirteenth century, associated with Debre Libanos Monastery, shown standing on one leg (his other leg is shown alongside, because of the tradition that it became detached from his having stood for so many years in prayer). St. George, slayer of the dragon, conqueror of evil, is also popular. Of the archangels, Michael and Gabriel attract the largest number of devotees. Pictures of the saints are not worshipped, neither are they used strictly as icons, but they are venerated for what they represent.

The Ethiopian Orthodox Church belongs to the Oriental Orthodox family of Christians, which also include the Egyptian Coptic, Armenian, Indian, and Syrian Churches. These Churches split from the rest of Christendom at the Council of Chalcedon in the fifth century. They are also known as miaphysite, or *Tewahido*, (in Ge'ez), because they describe Jesus Christ as "One incarnate nature of God the Word" (instead of "Two natures in One Person," a formula used by most other Christian Churches).

Christianity became the official religion of the Kingdom of Axum, northern Ethiopia, under King Ezana in about 330 CE. Tradition states that the faith was planted by two Christian brothers from Tyre, Frumentius and Edesius, who were shipwrecked on the coast. Frumentius was made the first bishop of the fledgling Church by Patriarch Athanasius in Egypt, and it was not until 1959 that the Ethiopian Orthodox Church became fully autonomous with the consecration of the first Ethiopian-born Patriarch, or *Abuna*. The Ethiopian Orthodox and Egyptian Coptic Churches are, in any case, very close in theology, liturgical style, and art.

By the end of the fifth century there was a renewal in the Church influenced by Syrian refugees, now known as the "Nine Saints." In the sixth century one of their disciples, St. Yared, who "learned his music from the birds," gave the Church its distinctive musical liturgy of chants, known as *zema*, in which the *debteras* (lay teachers and precentors) play an important role. Dressed in white garments they rattle the *sistra*, bang the drums, and dance as King David danced before the Holy of Holies. From about this time, too, churches were hewn from rocks and up cliff faces, many of them inhabited by hermits.

The Ethiopian Orthodox Church is also strongly marked by Jewish characteristics: Sabbath observance (although the main service is on a Sunday), the distinction between clean and unclean food, and circumcision rites. Ethiopian Christians also have a deep respect for the St. Mary of Zion church in Axum, where the original Ark of the Covenant is said to be housed, after being spirited away for safekeeping when Solomon's temple was destroyed in Jerusalem. Only the guardian of this most holy of relics is allowed to set eyes on it. Every Ethiopian church has its replica of this Ark of the Covenant, known as a *tabot*. As in Jewish tradition, it is around the *tabot* that worship takes place, normally in the building, but outside when paraded on certain feast days.

The Church also shares a history of coexistence with Islam. Islamic tradition states that the prophet Mohammed, in the sixth century, advised his followers to take refuge in Ethiopia because he knew the Axumite king treated foreigners kindly. Muslims and Christians in Ethiopia are mostly tolerant of one another and their adherents make pilgrimage to each other's shrines. Today there is a wariness in the relationship caused by events elsewhere.

Worship follows a weekly pattern of a Eucharist, in the form of a Liturgy (*Qidasse*), celebrated on Sundays. There is also a monthly cycle of saints' days, and an annual cycle of festivals that includes the main Church feasts of *Fasika* (Easter), *Timket* (Epiphany), and *Meskel* (Feast of the Exaltation of the Holy Cross). Services are led by several priests and many deacons, and often a choir with *debtera*. The priests alone are allowed behind an iconostasis inside the church, and they alone are allowed to handle the *tabot*.

The general public join in, or leave, at any point in the service, but only Orthodox are allowed communion. In practice, most people are seen worshiping outside the church building, and it is only the very young or very old who choose to take communion inside, because of the view that between those ages they are sexually impure.

Visitors are welcome in Orthodox churches, provided they leave their shoes at the door, cover their arms and legs, and respect the Church's traditions.

The Orthodox Church today is no longer tied to the State. It is now one of many Christian denominations, a factor that has had an influence on its internal dynamics and its sense of identity. Translations of the Bible into the major Ethiopian languages have led to a new renewal in the Church. There are theological colleges, and it takes its duty of caring for the poor seriously, with an administrative branch at the Synod office devoted to development projects.

MONASTIC LIFE

Monastic communities, both male and female, exist alongside the formal Church. They follow the pattern of the early Egyptian monasteries founded by the fourth-century saints Anthony and Pachomius. Many Ethiopian scholars were nurtured in monasteries, and the monasteries have been the preserve of literacy and manuscripts down the centuries. Some monasteries have had much influence in public life, for example, Debra Libanos Monastery, founded by St. Tekle Haimanot in the thirteenth century. It was St. Tekle Haimanot who helped to restore the Solomonic Emperors after the Zagwe dynasty failed. The abbot, or leader, of a

Inside Biete Gabriel-Rufael, one of the monolithic churches of Lalibela.

monastery is known as *Memher* (meaning "teacher" in Ge'ez, a title also applied to heads of large churches). Differing schools of theology developed in different monasteries, and these continue to provide subjects for debate today.

As in other Orthodox Churches only unmarried clergy are allowed to become bishops; these, and the Patriarch (*Abuna*) will be drawn from the rank of monks.

Although no longer influential in public life, monasteries continue to wield influence in the private lives of Ethiopians. Pilgrimages are made to monasteries for help with various troubles, such as sickness or barrenness. Holy water may be offered in bottles to take home as an efficacious cure. The most popular monasteries today are Debre Libanos, north of Addis Ababa; St. Mary of Zion in Axum, the oldest church and guardian of the Ark; the church of Egziabher Ab at Gishen Monastery, in Wollo, which has a fragment of the True Cross; and St. Gabriel of Kulubi, near Dire Dawa.

Most popular of all, of course, for those who can make it, is a pilgrimage to Jerusalem and a visit to the piece of Ethiopia that is the roof of the Church of the Holy Sepulchre—an area unfortunately hotly contested with the Egyptian Coptic Church. It is thought that the rock-hewn churches at Lalibela, with their allusions to Jerusalem, might have been built for those who could not make the journey to the real Jerusalem.

Men and women can join monasteries at any time of their lives. Many women will often join a community of nuns when they become widowed and no longer have anyone to look after them. In both cases, they wear distinctive saffron yellow dress.

FASTING

Fasting is commonly practiced in Ethiopia. The requirements are kept according to the strictness with which the faith is practiced.

Orthodox Ethiopians from puberty onward will fast on Wednesdays and Fridays. Most will also keep the longer fasts during Lent (fifty-six days), Advent (forty days), and Kweskwam, the Feast of the Flight to Egypt (forty days). As many as 250 days of the year can be kept as fast days. Fasting implies having only one meal a day, usually after 3:00 p.m., and abstaining from meat and dairy products. Fish can be eaten during fasting, which is why it is not considered fit for a celebratory meal. Lentils and beans, especially *misr wot* (lentil stew) or *shiro wot* (ground chickpea or bean stew) are the mainstays on fasting days.

Muslims fast during Ramadan, but this requires complete abstention from food or drink during the hours of daylight.

MAIN FEAST DAYS

In Ethiopia the Orthodox Church traditionally follows a calendar similar to the Julian calendar, as do Orthodox Churches elsewhere, which runs thirteen days behind

Timket (Epipheny) celebrations.

the Western, or Gregorian, calendar. As a result, Christmas and Epiphany in particular are celebrated later than in the West.

The most important Christian feast is Easter (*Fasika*), preceded by fifty-six days of fasting and daily services (*Hudade*, or *Abiy Tsom*). Its date is moveable and is always on or after the Western date of Easter. Christmas (*Lidet*, or *Genna*) is preceded by a forty day fast and occurs on January 7 (Western calendar). All fasts are broken by great feasting in which quantities of meat are consumed. Cows and sheep are vigorously traded in the days up to this point, and mounds of bloodstained skins and fleeces at marketplaces mark the changeover to a carnivorous diet.

The most colorful celebrations are Epiphany (*Timket*) and the Feast of the Finding of the True Cross

(*Meskel*) in late September. *Timket* celebrates the revelation of the divine Christ at his baptism in the Jordan River, whereas the Western Churches celebrate the revelation of Christ to the nations through the three wise men. On the evening before *Timket* the whole church, with its congregation and the priests, carrying the *tabot*, processes to the nearest river to keep vigil. The next day, accompanied by enthusiastic drumming and chanting, the faithful dip in the river to renew their own baptismal vows, and the priests sprinkle holy water over the crowds.

Meskel is enjoyed because it marks the end of the *kremt* rains and anticipates the harvest. Ethiopians believe St. Helena found the location of a part of the true cross by lighting a bonfire whose smoke returned to the place where the cross was buried. For this

A scene from the annual *Meskel* ceremony.

reason bonfires are a big feature of this feast, and ashes are marked on the foreheads of worshipers, and spread on fields to ensure good crops.

BAPTISM

Baptism is one of the sacraments of the Church, along with chrismation, penance, Holy Communion, the Unction of the Sick, matrimony, and Holy Orders. It marks the "rebirth" of a child into the Christian family. Baptism takes place forty days after the birth of a boy, or eighty days for a girl. The rite is long and includes the churching and purification of the mother. The child is anointed thirty times with holy oil all over its body; it is then dipped three times in water while the Holy Trinity is invoked. Godparents are appointed, as in Western Churches.

CATHOLIC CHRISTIANITY

Catholics are a significant minority of Christians. They have an archbishop based in Addis Ababa, and ten dioceses, including Adigrat in Tigray, and Endibir in the SNNP region. They follow both the western rite and the Ethiopic liturgical rite, using Ge'ez, and they are Chalcedonian in theology.

The presence of the Catholic Church in Ethiopia dates to the sixteenth-century Jesuit missions, which were caught up in politics as the Ethiopian emperors sought to fend off Muslim incursions. Later, Emperor Susenyos's conversion (*c.*1607–32) to Catholicism became a brief, but significant, interlude in the reign of Orthodoxy. The Orthodox clergy were horrified by this apostasy. Susenyos was deposed after a civil war, and the Jesuit missionaries were evicted from the country. Catholic missions did not reappear until 1839, when, under St. Justin de Jacobis, the Church embraced the Ethiopic rite. Italians in Eritrea later influenced the spread of Catholicism in Ethiopia, as well as a number of influential missions in the south, particularly at Endibir.

PROTESTANT CHRISTIANITY

Protestant Christianity is growing very fast, especially in the west and south of the country.

Protestant missionaries appeared in Ethiopia in the mid-nineteenth century. They sought not to convert, but to act as agents for reform in the Ethiopian Orthodox Church. Some of these early missionaries were held captive by Emperor Tewodros and made to design and build a large cannon for him. Such is the high regard in which Emperor Tewodros is now held in Ethiopia, that the largest of these cannons, nicknamed Sebastopol, has a replica in Tewodros Square, on Churchill Avenue, Addis Ababa.

Other missionaries from Scandinavia and America arrived from the early twentieth century, and were given permission to operate mostly in the southern half of the country, where Ethiopian Orthodoxy had not gained much of a foothold. The fruit of this work is the growth of two particularly large Churches: the Kale Hewot, which derives from mostly North American evangelical Christianity; and Mekane Yesus, which derives from mostly Scandinavian Lutheran Christianity. There are also a host of other Churches, many homegrown, and often charismatic in character.

Protestant theology, modern translations of the Bible into Amharic, and modern worship have sometimes influenced the Orthodox Church, and there are "reformed" Orthodox Churches in Addis Ababa, well-known for their Bible study and worship, especially among young people. However, change is not always well received in the Orthodox Church and some developments in the West, such as the ordination of women as priests, are resisted by many.

ISLAM

Islam in Ethiopia is as old as the religion itself. The walled city of Harar is considered the fourth most holy city in Islam after Mecca, Medina, and Jerusalem, with 82 mosques and 102 shrines. The Prophet Mohammed advised those of his followers in Mecca who were being persecuted to go to northern Ethiopia, where they would "find a king who does not wrong anyone." These people later settled in Negash, Tigray, in 615 CE, now considered the home of Islam in East Africa. Both Muslims and Christians respect each other's shrines, the most important Islamic one being the twelfth-century Sheikh Hussein mosque to the east of the Bale Mountains.

However, relations were not always so sweet. In the sixteenth century a warlord, Mohammed Gragn, from the rising Emirate of Adal, nearly succeeded in overrunning the Christian kingdoms to the north, but was thwarted by a combined Ethio–Portuguese army. Later, the Ottoman Empire threatened Ethiopia's interests when it took the Red Sea coastal ports. The supposed conversion of Emperor Iyasu to Islam, in the early twentieth century, was one of the factors that led to his deposition. Today, relations on a personal level are mostly tolerant, though there are occasional reports of conflict in rural areas where one religion poses a threat in the community to the other. At a national level there is unease because of the threat from Islamic extremism in Somalia; and Saudi Arabian Wahabism, and its underwriting of mosques in town and country, is greeted with suspicion by all Christians.

CIRCUMCISION

Circumcision is widely practiced on both boys and girls. Circumcision for boys is, uniquely in Christian churches, practiced as a rite in Ethiopian Orthodoxy eight days after birth (another Jewish custom), and also among Muslims. Female circumcision is against the law in Ethiopia, but the law is not strongly enforced. Ethiopia has not yet ratified the African Union's Maputo Protocol (2005) against the practice.

TRADITIONAL BELIEFS

Apart from the three monotheistic religions, animistic beliefs and practices are to be found in Ethiopia, mainly

in the south and west, and among the Oromo, and much syncretism of traditional beliefs with the main religions. Animism is practiced by tribal peoples, but there is also widespread practice of sorcery, divination, and astrology, particularly among rural people. Charms hung around the neck to ward off evil spirits, recourse to divining coffee dregs or fat from animals, are all encountered in places where life is most insecure and uncertain.

WEDDINGS

Marriages are made legal at a civil ceremony. Although men often marry late in life, women can marry very young. The legal age is 18 years, but this can drop to 16 years with parental consent. The law is not always enforced and girls as young as 11 years can find themselves married and sexually active. Such girls can experience complications in childbirth.

All ethnic groups and religions have their own customs to mark betrothals and weddings. Few Christians have a ceremony in church because of the strict conditions the Church sets for marriage: divorce is not allowed by those married in church, for example, and Ethiopians traditionally have had a liberal view of divorce and remarriage. Marriages are usually negotiated

between the two families by a mediator, a role also used by diaspora Ethiopians who seek a wife from home.

When a wedding takes place, it is a protracted affair that can take several days, during which there is a boisterous and noisy cavalcade of hooting cars. Pride of place goes to the cameraman perched in a car that drives back and forth to catch every moment. Woe betide those who get in the way. Westerners can be invited to any part of the wedding, though it is likely to be for the main meal and the dancing that follows. (See more on page 123.)

The giving of presents by guests is not as common in Ethiopia as in the West. The pinning of money to the bridal couple for luck during dancing at the reception is done, but not at very posh weddings. The bridegroom presents the bride with a trousseau of dresses, to which she is supposed to express scorn, while accepting them nevertheless.

In the Oromo countryside you might come across a wedding celebration. You'll see a party of traditional horsemen, their steeds ornately and colorfully saddled and bridled, galloping about in good-natured drunkenness.

FUNERALS

A white tent pitched in the street alongside a house is a sure sign of a funeral. These are very important events that involve the whole community. The family will probably be a member of an *idir*, a self-help funeral insurance club, which mobilizes to make decisions and pay the funeral costs.

When a person dies, mourners gather at the deceased's home to comfort the family and make arrangements. The tent (*denkwan*) is ordered to provide seating space, the women will generally prepare food for the mourners, and the men will make other practical arrangements such as ordering the coffin. The burial takes place within a day or two of death, in a graveyard near the church, and is conducted by a priest, if Christian. The *denkwan* will remain for several more days to enable all the mourners to pay their respects. It is usual to make a point of greeting the most closely bereaved, then to sit quietly and somberly in chairs placed around the *denkwan* for a suitable length of time, and then quietly take your leave after you have been offered something to eat.

It is worth noting that the *idir* is a very important social grouping in its own right. They gather members together regularly to make decisions about funds, and the funds themselves might also be used for times of hardship, or credit.

All Ethiopians, not just Christians, are buried quickly after death. Wealthy Christians mark their graves with large headstones or mausoleums. Oromo are buried in colorful graves in the countryside, often decorated with birds and animals. The Konso in the south are animists and their wooden funeral statues are well-known. Muslims are buried in their own graveyards. There is a foreign cemetery with sections for Armenians, Greeks, and other Europeans—including those who died during the fighting to liberate Ethiopia in 1941—in Gulele on the western outskirts of Addis Ababa.

COFFEE CEREMONY AND STIMULANTS

The taking of coffee at an Ethiopian home is an unhurried, elaborate ritual. Although the custom of drinking hot, roasted coffee is thought to have been invented in Arabia, such is the pride Ethiopians have for Arabica coffee— which has its origins in the country and is now its biggest export—that legends have grown around it.

Every woman, and many men, is practiced at roasting coffee. On special occasions rushes are spread about the floor and decorated with flowers. The washed green beans are roasted dry in a pan over a hot brazier. When the beans crackle, the smoke is wafted toward the guests to whet their senses, and incense is burned to mingle with the smoke. When ready, the roasted beans are taken away and pounded in a mortar.

Meanwhile, water is put to boil in a clay coffeepot (*jebena*) and the coffee is brewed in the same pot. It is then carefully poured into twelve small cups, representing the apostles. Sugar, and occasionally salt, are added to taste. Visitors should try to accept three pourings: the first is known as *abol* in Amharic, the second *huletegna*, and the third is the blessing, known as *bereka*. Roasted peanuts or barley (*kollo*) are handed around to accompany the coffee.

Much older is the custom of mashing coffee leaves or roasted beans, and mixing the grounds with butter. This is then used as a stimulant by travelers, or by monks needing to pray all night.

Chat (also transliterated as *khat*, or *qat*, especially in Arabic), a stimulant containing amphetamine, is

widely grown and used and is also one of the highest value exports. It is normally chewed as part of a social ritual among Muslims in Yemen and Somalia, as well as in Ethiopia. It grows where coffee grows and it is now chewed more widely, particularly by the younger generation, to help them through exams or hardship. For this reason, *chat* is often disapproved of. *Chat* is illegal in the USA, Canada, and many parts of Europe.

TIME AND CALENDAR

Ethiopia traditionally follows the Coptic calendar still in use in Egypt, and uses an era that is seven years and eight months behind the Western Gregorian calendar. On September 12, 2007, Ethiopia celebrated its new millennium.

The extra five days tagged onto the twelve thirty-day months of the Coptic calendar is reckoned as a "thirteenth month." Take care when using government documents as they all use the Coptic calendar.

The time of day is also reckoned differently. This follows the traditional Middle Eastern twelve-hour clock, when the hours are counted from dawn, being 6:00 a.m. Thus 9:00 a.m. is three o'clock in Ethiopia, and twelve noon is six o'clock.

Aware of these differences, Ethiopians will usually remember when talking with foreigners to be precise about which calendar or timing they are using. Reference to the Western, or European, calendar is made; and to Ethiopian or European time when the clock is mentioned.

CHAPTER FOUR

MAKING FRIENDS

Ethiopians value long-term friendships. These often go back to childhood and school days, and extend beyond family, tribe, and religious background. An Ethiopian friendship requires and exhibits deep loyalty, and may well involve the sharing of all kinds of material resources, such as cars and houses, as well as the less demanding expectations of attendance at weddings, funerals, and other family events. In the event of grave sickness or other serious family trouble, an established friendship will require one to drop everything, and make oneself available to help in whatever way is needed.

ETHIOPIANS AND FOREIGNERS

Making friends is apparently easy at a superficial level, but deeper relationships will require interaction over a number of years. Friendships between Ethiopians and foreigners are frequent, and longstanding foreign residents can expect to find themselves wholly integrated into the community. However, Ethiopians and foreigners who become friends occasionally do experience disappointment if expectations of what is to be gained from that friendship differ.

Ethiopians have a long established culture of care of guests. This can involve simple kindnesses, like an invitation to a foreigner to share, or the offer to pay for, a cup of coffee, a glass of beer, or a soft drink. They may be disappointed if this approach is not reciprocated. On the other hand, only people with an ulterior motive will offer too much too soon. Be wary of anyone who seems to be too pressing in their attempts to build a friendship; they may be trying to box you into position where you cannot say no to a request for an expensive favor.

When entering into relationships with foreigners, Ethiopians are also often a little wary. It is as well to remember that Ethiopians may regard foreigners as technically and sometimes materially superior, but they will also regard Western culture as morally inferior to their own, particularly in its inadequate sense of family loyalty, and its attitude to old people. Since some Westerners come to Ethiopia in order to "do good" among people who are poor, and some come with their own, unacknowledged, sense of moral superiority, a clash can occur in the interaction between Ethiopian and Westerner.

INVITATIONS HOME

If you receive an invitation to an Ethiopian home for a meal, you can safely take a cake or flowers as a present. In return, expect an Ethiopian to present you with a cake bought from a patisserie when visiting your home.

Ethiopians, whoever they are, are not shy of inviting foreigners to their homes, and evenings and weekends after work are usually the chosen times. In more traditional homes, wives will do the cooking, but not take part in the meal, with any children or servants helping. At the very least, coffee is usually offered and, depending on the level of the invitation, this is done as a ceremony with the coffee being roasted on a brazier in front of the guests, and grass and flowers placed on the floor in their honor. The conversation at such times can often follow intellectual discussions on such topics as religion, philosophy, and politics, and the fortunes of Manchester United and Arsenal football (soccer) clubs. If food is offered, it will be traditional Ethiopian, with *injera* (a type of flatbread) and various *wots* (stews). Western bread, and non-spicy foods, may also be offered, specially prepared for a foreign guest, but appreciation of Ethiopian food will be welcomed.

It is good manners, in dealing with *injera* and *wot* meals, to use only the right hand to eat with, as the left is considered unclean. It is also common practice to leave a small piece of *injera* uneaten on your plate when you have finished, to show that you have had your fill. If you do not do this, you may be pressed to eat more than you want. It is also sometimes the custom for an Ethiopian host to feed his guests by hand, preparing a small roll of *injera* with *wot*, and putting it directly in the guest's mouth. If this is unwelcome, it is enough to explain that it is not your custom, to avoid giving offense.

HOW DO YOU MEET ETHIOPIANS?

Ethiopians are ready enough to talk to complete strangers, but genuine friendships most often begin with an introduction, or with a common professional or business interest. Foreigners and Ethiopians work together in a variety of contexts—business, academic, medical, technical, and diplomatic.

It is also possible to meet ordinary people in bars, hotels, and restaurants, but you will need to be aware of the status of the place you are meeting in. Addis Ababa has a huge variety of restaurants, bars, and nightclubs. Expectations of what you will encounter in them can be confusing to the newcomer.

MEN AND WOMEN—CROSS-CULTURAL RELATIONSHIPS

Intermarriage between Ethiopians and foreigners is not at all unusual, especially between Ethiopian women and men from the Eastern Mediterranean, who have been settling in the country for centuries. Romance and marriage between Ethiopians and other foreigners is also becoming increasingly common. These relationships are often very happy and successful, though of course they can and do incur cross-cultural strains. For example, Western women can find that their husband's relatives from the countryside outstay their welcome, and they also come in very large numbers. They will also find that the terms "aunt," "uncle," "sister," and "brother" are expanded to include many other extended family members, as well as those adopted into the family. The same courtesy should be given to them as to close family members. On the other hand, an Ethiopian woman can find her foreign husband's unwillingness to support older members of the family— for instance by inviting his mother-in-law to join them in their home in the West—very galling indeed.

There are also a number of marriages between older Western men and much younger Ethiopian women. The Ethiopian wife in this case may have ambitions to find economic security, and be affronted if this is not on offer. In parallel with this are the cases of very young Ethiopian men who marry older foreign women, and become rapidly disillusioned if a visa and move to the West do not materialize quite soon after the wedding.

In contemplating these things, the visitor to Ethiopia needs to be aware that marriage here is not always a lifelong relationship. Exploitative relationships between men and women are no more unknown in Ethiopian culture than they are in the West. Gay relationships are frowned upon and are illegal; LGBT travelers are advised to practice great discretion.

LOW LIFE

All Ethiopian towns have bars, euphemistically translated in Amharic as *buna bet*, or "coffeehouse." Respectable women are almost never to be seen in these bars, some of which double up as brothels or hotels. There will be plenty of alcohol on sale, and perhaps not much coffee. A male traveler who gets sexually involved with a prostitute does so at his peril; sexually transmitted infections, among them AIDS, are not uncommon.

It is possible that a visitor may be invited to a *chat* chewing session. The Muslim tradition of chewing *chat* has spread throughout the whole Ethiopian community. *Chat* is a shrub (*Catha edulis*), from which fresh clippings are taken daily. When chewed, it acts as mild narcotic due to amphetamine-like substances in the plant, bringing energy and elation to begin with, somnolence and confusion later. Chewing *chat* is common, but not, except perhaps in Harar culture, a particularly respectable activity. A visitor can say no to this and little offense will be taken.

AVOIDING EXPLOITATION IN RELATIONSHIPS

Relationships between equals often work the best. This rules out exploitation by inducing feelings of guilt about material inequality, and is generally attainable between Ethiopians and foreigners who know each other well, whatever their material, educational, or social status.

There are, however, some relationships that become exploitative. Ethiopians and foreigners have different ways of exploiting each other. Some foreigners, who make friends in order to find a business partner, to find romance, or to get around the country, mistake the loyalty of Ethiopians in friendship and forget to offer reciprocal courtesies, or that Ethiopians also need to balance the demands of their homes and families with time spent with their foreign friends.

There are some foreigners who employ Ethiopian girls as domestics for very low wages and expect a high level of service over very long hours. There is little personal relationship on offer. In Ethiopia, domestic servants expect to be treated on human terms, and may well invite you to their homes. You should reciprocate at least by getting to know employees personally, and by offering fair wages and fair treatment. They will appreciate a gift on your return from abroad, and a tip from any guests who are staying with you.

Ethiopians often exploit Westerners by various forms of begging. This can range from begging in the street or in traffic lines, to requests for money delivered by letter or at a prearranged private meeting. You may find yourself having to deal with the flattering suggestion that only you can understand, because of your especially compassionate nature, the particular difficulties of the person making the request. It is a mistake to fall for this kind of flattery. You can safely say "No."

GREETINGS AND FAREWELLS

Ethiopians greet their friends and family, including their foreign friends, in various ways, often with an embrace, a touching of shoulders, or a kiss on each cheek, and again on the first side, if they have not seen each other for a long time, but always at least by shaking hands. It is conventional for each party to ask the other if they are well, and to reply that they are (even if they are not!), and to add "*Egziabher Yimesgen,*" which means "Thanks be to God." Muslims often prefer to say "*Alhamdulillah,*" which means the same thing in Arabic.

When you arrive back in the country after a long period away, your Ethiopian friends will often greet you warmly, welcoming you back into your place in their social network. When returning overseas, friends may insist on giving you a present, often a souvenir of Ethiopia, to take home with you—it might be T-shirts for your children, or a bag of coffee for you to drink in your own country.

Saying goodbye generally involves a form of words meaning "be well"—in Amharic, *Dehna hunu.* If you have been visiting Ethiopians at home, they will generally come to the door, to your car, or the gate of their compound to see you out. Doing this is called *meshenyet,* or "accompanying," in Amharic. If you are leaving Ethiopia for good after a long stay, you may find a large meal has been prepared for you as a farewell and people will come with you to the airport to see you off as they would their own families.

CHAPTER FIVE

THE ETHIOPIANS AT HOME

THE HOME AND THE COMPOUND

Ethiopians favor the traditional compound (or enclosure) as a model for their home life. It provides security and room for their extended family to share a common life.

In the Ethiopian countryside a family will live in a thatched house built of mud and wood, or stone, and almost always surrounded by a wall, or a fence with a gateway. There may be two or three houses within the enclosure, belonging to members of an extended family. The enclosure is known as a *gebi* in Amharic, and this is always translated in English as "compound."

This pattern has been adapted to fit the urban lifestyle of Addis Ababa and other large towns, where middle-class people build themselves a family home, surrounded by a wall or a fence, with a big front gate. This constitutes a compound. Current planning

A modern home in Addis Ababa.

regulations in Addis Ababa, where land is scarce, favor a multistory building, with a very small compound, but houses that go back twenty-five years or more are likely to be one-story villas with a rather larger garden space.

Poorer people in the cities will rent one or two rooms in a compound owned by a private landlord, or by the *kebele*, roughly equivalent to a community council, the lowest unit of local government in both city and countryside. This kind of accommodation is rapidly being replaced by condominiums, blocks of apartments built to a standard design. Urban society is still adjusting to the changes in lifestyle these apartments entail.

A mother and her children in Tigray.

THE FAMILY

The family unit in Ethiopia extends to brothers and sisters and their children, sons and daughters who have not been able to establish themselves in their own home, and their spouses and children. City families tend to be smaller than countryside ones, with two children often seen as a comfortable and affordable number. Elderly parents may also be accommodated in the family home. Middle-class families are also likely to have some live-in servants, and there may be a separate series of rooms at the back of the compound for them.

Most modern homes will have a living room with a few armchairs, or a sofa surrounding a low table, and if there is room, a dining table with upright chairs. Almost everybody aspires to own a television, and this will be prominent in the living room. The traditional dining table in Ethiopia is a *mesob*, a three-foot-high (ninety-centimeter-high) basket with a shallow rim, fitted to a basket ware base, in which a tray containing *injera* and *wot* can be placed. Even if this is not regularly used in a modern household, it is likely that there will be one somewhere on display in the living room. In the kitchen, or in a cabinet with cups on display, will be all the equipment needed for making food, including the means for roasting and brewing coffee in the traditional manner. In a modern home the cooking facility is likely to be electricity or propane gas, or there will be a small brazier using charcoal, or a Chinese-made kerosene stove, which can be placed on the floor.

Eating together is an important part of Ethiopian life. Given that people, in town and country, need to rise early and leave for work early, they will often take a light breakfast, have their lunch either at an eating house, or out of a lunch box, and then have a family meal at about 7:00 p.m. Most people will expect to be in bed by 9:30 p.m.

The family home will also be decorated with religious pictures, or biblical texts, and family photographs. There may also be artificial or real flowers around the house, particularly in the Ethiopian spring after the rains in September.

LIFE'S ROUTINES

Orthodox Christians are regular churchgoers. Many will have a close link to a church dedicated to a particular saint or archangel, and they will attend that church early on Sunday mornings, and on regular church festivals.

If they belong to a *mehaber*, a church-based association, each member will provide hospitality for the other members, and receive hospitality from them in turn, on a regular basis. A *mehaber* can also function as a savings club, called *ikub*, and as a funeral society, so that the cost of a funeral, and the hospitality costs associated with it, does not fall on a single family at a time of bereavement. The *ikub* members all contribute a fixed sum every month to a central kitty, and then each takes the whole kitty when it is their turn to do so. This works as a form of life assurance, or micro-finance bank.

Catholic and Protestant Christians will also devote their Sundays to Church activities. Protestants, however, do not usually observe saints' days, and do not generally observe the fasting regulations of the Church.

Muslims will generally attend Friday midday prayers at the mosque, and will also observe Ramadan. As Sunday remains the official day of rest, they may go out to lunch at a restaurant, or on a picnic that day. Picnics, if taken, are generally at a park outside town, or in an enclosure just on the edge of a main road, enhanced with flower beds and chairs and tables.

In the countryside, attendance at markets, which happen weekly, or sometimes twice weekly in small towns, is a social as well as a commercial activity. Many of these towns take their names from their market day—for example, "Thursday Market"—and the townspeople provide services for those who come to it. Sellers and buyers may often have to walk many miles to reach the market, and if they do well on a sale, they will often refresh themselves for the walk home with a glass or two of *tella*, a drink made from barley that is similar to beer, or *tej*, a stronger alcoholic drink made from fermented honey.

In Addis Ababa markets are important too. The main market of Addis Ababa, called the Mercato, is

A market in Oromia.

Women shop for cloth in Axum.

said to be Africa's largest market, and is home to one of the city's most important business communities. There are also smaller markets in various parts of the city with covered stalls selling most of what might be needed in the kitchen. At various points are places where sheep and goats are also traded. These smaller markets are located on the periphery of the city center.

DAILY WORK

Most middle-class Ethiopian families can only get by if both husband and wife are working. This means that everybody gets up early, the children are packed off to school, and the adults are in a taxi or a bus by about 7:30 a.m.

If the family is wealthy enough, or is joined by a young relative from the countryside, there will be a servant or two to manage the household, usually female. This person is responsible for preparing breakfast, sweeping floors, washing clothes (usually by hand), and buying ingredients from the local market, kiosk, or small supermarket. Meat is bought fresh from a butcher who has slaughtered it according to the required Christian or Muslim ritual, or on the hoof. Chickens are usually bought live, then killed and plucked at home.

Evenings may be spent helping children with their

homework or watching television. On weekends there is time for sports or a visit to a park.

In the countryside, much depends on the agricultural season, whether it is plowing, planting, or harvesting time. No one is idle for long for everything is done by hand, from taking stones out of a pile of beans, to sorting the seeds from last year's harvest into categories that maximize their growing potential for the next.

Gatherings at churches are often social, with *talla* (beer) dispensed, and a chance for government development workers to impart messages about the environment or agricultural innovation. Rivers, too, provide opportunities for women to socialize while washing their clothes, or collecting water; there, they meet their friends, pass gossip, and reinforce bonds. If a woman finds her domestic work for the day is finished she will then likely be making handicrafts, such as weaving a colored basket. Boys, often as young as five, are usually given the responsible task of looking after the family's animals while they graze outside the compound. At night they are brought into the compound to protect them from theft or wild animals.

GROWING UP IN ETHIOPIA

In town or country, every family will hope to send their children to school, hopefully for the complete twelve-year syllabus, but certainly for the eight years of primary and junior secondary. There was a time when girls would drop out of school earlier than boys because of either early marriage, or the need for them to help domestically, but in much of Ethiopia this is no longer the case.

The state provides free education, and both in the countryside and in Addis Ababa capacity constraints have led to a shift system, in which each classroom is used for two shifts by day, and for evening classes as well. Children will walk up to nine miles (fifteen kilometers) a day to attend school. Private education is developing fast, and many families in the major cities will go to great lengths to pay for this in order to get a longer school day, and for the possibility of learning English. Private schools run a regular school day from about 9:00 a.m. to about 3:30 p.m. Middle-class parents generally hire a taxi or a shared minibus to take their children to school.

Recent years have seen a huge expansion in the provision of both state and private higher education. Many Ethiopian families also now wish to provide this opportunity for their children, which means that offspring of college age often continue to live at home, or with relatives in the larger towns, until well into their twenties. Wealthier families often look for a university

education abroad for their children, in India, in Europe, or in North America. Universities in Ethiopia, both private and state funded, are expanding every year.

Service in the army, which is no longer compulsory, provides opportunities for young people from the countryside to get away from home, and join the wider Ethiopian society.

MARRIAGE

There are two quite different patterns for marriage in Ethiopia, the traditional and the modern. In modern Addis Ababa, and in the bigger cities, people get married at almost any age between twenty and fifty. Men in particular will leave the decision to get married until they are economically established, and this may take a long time. Many urban women find it quite hard to find a partner, and some remain unmarried for life. Young people will expect to choose their own partner, and they will not expect their families to interfere with their choice. Online dating apps are most commonly used by affluent city, or diaspora, Ethiopians. When they do get married, they may convert from the Christian faith to Islam, or vice versa; this is now quite acceptable among educated people.

In the countryside the traditional pattern persists. Young men expect to marry and set up a home at eighteen or younger and their brides are often as young as eleven, though this is not legal. Although there is official discouragement of this practice from both secular and religious authorities, it still persists despite the dangers, for example, of childbirth before the girl has fully grown up. Arranged marriages do occur, particularly for daughters in their very early teens, often to much older men, and largely for economic reasons—sometimes girls run away from home to the cities to avoid such marriages. Most marriages are monogamous; polygamous Islamic and pagan marriages do take place but are less common than they used to be.

As we have seen, marriage ceremonies, whether in town or countryside, have certain common elements. In the city there will be processions of cars and limousines, decorated with ribbons and flowers, to collect the bride from her home, bring her to the ceremony, to take the newly married couple for photographs in a park, and then on to a reception. At the reception there will be tables groaning with food, including raw meat, supplied in the form of a carcass, from which a butcher will chop a helping for each guest to be eaten raw.

In the countryside there will be brightly caparisoned horses instead of vehicles, and a blowing of brass trumpets instead of car horns. The reception will be held in a tent rather than a hotel, but the basic pattern of the ceremony will be the same.

A priest may be on hand to add a blessing, but only committed Orthodox Christians will be married in church. In that case the religious ceremony will take place during the early morning liturgy on a Saturday or Sunday, and all the rest of the proceedings will follow.

DEATH AND MOURNING

A funeral is always a significant occasion, and the whole community will attend. In the countryside this means a whole village or small town joining in. In cities it means friends and family, and work colleagues, of the deceased. There are no cremations. Orthodox and Protestant Christians, and Muslims, are buried in separate cemeteries.

After the burial, the mourning tent will be put up, in which food and drink will be served to the mourners. For several days afterward bereaved members of the family will sit in it and receive the condolences of friends and relatives. Most will come and sit in silence, or converse in low voices for between thirty and sixty minutes. If a foreigner or a visitor has had any kind of relationship with the person who has died, then they should at least attend and sit in the tent for a brief time. Flowers should not be brought or sent to a funeral in Ethiopia.

People will wear black for up to a year following the death of a close relative.

THE YEAR'S ROUND

As we have seen, Ethiopia follows a calendar of Coptic, or Egyptian, origin and the routine follows both religious and agricultural cycles.

The major festivals are public holidays, and are occasions for people to visit their hometown for a few days, or to stay at home with family. These include New Year, on September 11; *Meskel*, on September 29, which coincides with the end of the *kremt*, the season of the big rains; Christmas, on January 7; and Epiphany, on January 19. The Oromo spring festival of Ireecha in October has become more prominent in recent years. Easter and the major Muslim festivals have moveable dates. Besides attending church services and religious ceremonies during these festivals, people will celebrate by breaking their fast, whether of Lent or Ramadan, and eating meat. Families will buy a chicken or a sheep, or take a share in an ox, and these animals will be slaughtered early in the morning of the day of the festival.

People will also sometimes visit a vacation resort for a festival. The nearest thing that Ethiopia has to a beach resort is the shore of Lake Langano, in the Rift Valley. Now crowded with hotels, this offers a place to swim or lie in the sun. Other favorite resorts for Addis Ababa residents are at the crater lakes of Bishoftu, an hour's drive to the south, or Sodere, a couple of miles south of Adama (or Nazareth), where hot springs feed straight into a swimming pool.

Apart from festivals, Ethiopians seem to take few vacations, often accumulating several months of annual leave over several years, and then perhaps taking three months off to visit a relative or friend in America or Europe.

In the countryside, the rhythms of agriculture are more significant. The fields are plowed before the big rains (*kremt*) in May, and sown with grain crops in

June or July, so that they will ripen after the rains end in September. They will then be harvested, threshed, and winnowed by December. Other crops—such as lentils, chickpeas, and beans—follow their own cycle, but all will be complete by Christmas, or soon after. During the long, dry, hot months that follow, nothing much can be sown unless there are satisfactory short rains in March or April, or unless an adjacent river provides irrigation possibilities. In this situation people grow crops of pumpkin, onions, or tomatoes.

The question asked every year is whether there will be short rains, and whether they will be sufficient for a harvest before the big rains in July.

In the south and west, coffee prices and annual yields are crucial to millions of people. Some years produce a bumper crop, other years do not. World prices go up and down and, with modern communications, even the remotest growers are aware of what their product is worth from day to day. The beginning of the new coffee harvest each year after the rains is important to all, from small scale farmers to the government anxiously hoping for foreign exchange.

DRESS

A throng of people at a market or outside a church will mostly be wearing white: shawls, head scarves, dresses, and men's jodhpurs, mostly made from locally woven cotton. Only in Muslim and lowland areas, such as Harar, is there more color.

Although Western dress is the norm in the cities, and is replacing traditional rural dress, on special occasions all Ethiopians revert to the traditional style, sometimes updated. Women wear a basic long white cotton kaftan, drawn at the waist by a colored tie, and an embroidered inset around the bottom. Depending on wealth or status, the embroidery is wider and more ornate. Every Ethiopian woman will have a selection of dresses, often provided as a trousseau on marriage.

A man's smart dress is also white: a pair of white jodhpurs, or loose trousers, with a short white kaftan on top, and the outfit is finished with white shoes. The

Women in traditional white kaftans.

only colors to creep into this all-white attire are likely to be those of the Ethiopian flag—red, green, and yellow—which may be sewn into a seam or around the brim of a hat.

A shawl thrown around the shoulders or over the head, also of white cotton, known as a *shama* ("woven"), is worn mostly by women. The thicker *gabi* is essential in the cooler highlands.

In the city, where Western fashion prevails, women are happy to wear tight jeans and fashionable shoes, and the attitude is relaxed; jackets and ties for men are rarely worn unless for very special meetings.

All children wear school uniform, which, for girls, is generally a modest ankle-length skirt. Muslim women will invariably wear a longer skirt and a head scarf.

DRINKING COFFEE

Coffee is Ethiopia's national beverage. People believe that it takes its Western name from the province of Kafa in southwest Ethiopia, and that it was "discovered" for the world by an Ethiopian goatherd named Kaldi. Coffee in Amharic is *buna*, and, as we have seen, the drinking of it is accompanied by much custom and ceremony. It is drunk throughout Ethiopia, with coffee houses in every town, and is served up by street vendors. Village women will invite each other to drink it just as eagerly as middle-class women in Addis Ababa. It is always served after a meal with guests—spiced, without milk, and with large spoonfuls of sugar if desired.

CHAPTER SIX

TIME OUT

Leisure activities in Ethiopia vary from traditional games, to modern sports, to intellectual sparring over a glass of whiskey. What people choose to do largely depends on whether they live in the city or the countryside, and how much income they have to spare. Coffeehouses abound throughout the country and are where both men and women will spend time socializing with friends, talking and relaxing over coffee or a soda. Restaurants in towns host evening trysts, and parks are popular for walks with family and friends. Ethiopians are also spending an increasing amount of time keeping up with friends and family on social media and messaging apps such as WhatsApp, Viber, and Telegram.

Traditional games like *Gabeta* (a board game played with stones and a number of holes), and Ethiopian chess, were once played regularly in the home. Today, in towns, they have given way to television, which will often be on in the corner of a room as much for its background sound as for actual viewing. Television

screens are also in view in bars, hotels, and other
public places—useful for those who cannot afford a
television at home. Satellite television, featuring CNN
and international sports channels, is often available in
the most remote locations. The fortunes of top English
and Italian soccer teams are followed throughout the
land. In the countryside, games of ping pong or table
soccer are played on tables outside in many main
streets of small towns.

Those who live outside of the cities are more
likely to combine social and traditional pursuits with
religious and national holidays. Family or community
obligations, such as weddings and funerals, are
de rigueur. Particularly religious individuals will
make time for devotions to their favorite saint or
go on pilgrimage.

Ethiopians are not at all shy of inviting foreigners
to join them at home, especially for family events and
on religious days. In turn, they, with their sense of
curiosity, will gladly accept a foreigner's invitation to
a meal at their home, a concert, or a foray to a tourist
site out of town. However, since urban Ethiopians
on the whole prefer bright lights to the silence of the
countryside, they might prefer a visit to a spa or town
outside Addis Ababa to hiking up a bare mountainside.
It is always worth asking, however, as there will be
exceptions to this generalization.

Although individuals largely dislike being
photographed in an ordinary context, they do not
mind if you are taking photographs of them at a
major festival.

PUBLIC HOLIDAYS

Ethiopians enjoy thirteen public holidays, celebrating Christian or Islamic holy days and important national events.

September 11: New Year's Day in the Ethiopian calendar (St. John's Day). Marked by bonfires and a holiday

September 27: Feast of *Meskel*, which celebrates the finding of the true cross in Jerusalem by St. Helena, and the end of the rains

January 7: Christmas (*Lidetta*), preceded by fasting

January 19: Epiphany, or the Baptism of Christ (*Timket*). An especially colorful ceremony during which priests parade the churches' *tabots* around a pool or stream, and sprinkle the crowd with holy water

March 2: Victory at Adwa Day. A secular holiday celebrating Menelik II's victory over the Italians in 1896

March to April: Good Friday and Easter Day, moveable feasts, usually later than their Western equivalents, and the most important Christian days, preceded by a long fast

May 1: International Labor Day

May 5: Ethiopian Patriots' Victory Day, which marks the downfall of the Italian Fascist occupation in 1941

May 28: Downfall of the Derg Regime in 1991

The Muslim festivals of *Id al-Fitre* (marking the end of *Ramadan*), *Id al-Adha* (Feast of Sacrifice), and *Maulid* (which celebrates the Prophet Mohammed's birthday), follow dates in the Islamic lunar calendar and are celebrated a few weeks earlier every year.

AFTER WORK AND WEEKENDS

For Ethiopians in employment, weekends and evenings are a time for regrouping and relaxing. It will be a time to be with their school-age children or, if unmarried, a time to be with friends, and go to a café or a bar. Many people who are trying to better themselves with extra qualifications will often take the opportunity to put in extra study, or go to night school. The spread of excellent museums throughout the country has provided Ethiopians with another opportunity to both admire their country's achievements and history, and educate themselves.

How one socializes after work in Addis Ababa is divided along class and religious lines. Protestants will not drink at all, whereas affluent Orthodox Christians think nothing of celebrating with alcohol. Shisha bars have become popular in wealthy parts of town, especially Bole. Selling shisha is however illegal and bars are the occasional targets of police raids after tough legislation introduced in 2015 saw smoking in public areas and the sale of flavored tobacco both banned.

Shopping is by and large not a leisure activity except for those who can afford it. Cash is still used for payment in most places, though cards are becoming more common. Mobile payment apps are making inroads; CBE Birr, an app developed by the Commercial Bank of Ethiopia, is the most frequently used.

WEDDINGS AND FAMILY EVENTS

Weddings, we have seen, are major social events. There will normally be a ceremony of some sort in church or a hotel, followed by a drive about the city in convoy, all captured on video. This will be followed by the reception, with tables laden with food, including raw meat. There will also be a band and normally a soloist singing traditional songs. A few days later there will be a second reception (*mels*), traditionally hosted by the bride's family.

If you are invited to a wedding, do dress smartly, go easy on the *tej* (honey wine), and enjoy taking part in the dancing, particularly the traditional shoulder-led *eskista* dance. You do not need to take a present, but there may be a dance in which banknotes are pinned to the clothes of the bride and groom.

Ethiopians only reluctantly leave their children behind when they attend a social occasion, and young children can be seen late into the night in restaurants. Middle-class Ethiopians will also lavish attention and money on children's birthday parties.

MENAFESHA

Ethiopians like taking the air. There are many recreation parks, known as *Menafesha*—literally, a place for getting fresh air—generally on the outskirts of a town or city, where people go to relax, enjoy beer or fizzy drinks, and sometimes music. There will be trees and flowering shrubs, and tables and chairs under a gazebo or awning of some sort; and they will vary from the very posh to a simple affair for those with less cash to spare. Weddings and other parties can be held at a *Menafesha*, or they may call in at one between the ceremony and the meal, for photographs among the flowers. Some *Menafesha* have merry-go-rounds and swings for children.

SPAS

Ethiopians love their hot water spas. Addis Ababa was built near a spa, known by the Oromo name, Finfinne (*Filwoha* in Amharic), which the Empress Taitu patronized at the end of the nineteenth century. This now supplies hot water for public baths, graded and priced accordingly, where a bath followed by a traditional Ethiopian meal can be had. Swimming pools at both the Hilton and Ghion hotels in Addis Ababa are heated by hot springs.

Outside Addis Ababa, the resorts popular with Ethiopians are at Sodere, near Adama, with its two heated swimming pools, and at Ambo, two hours' drive west of Addis Ababa, and the home of one of Ethiopia's first bottled mineral waters—now generic for sparkling water. Middle-class Ethiopians might go for a weekend with their children, or a group of unmarried Ethiopians. For those who do not have a car, it is often the choice for a bus outing.

Injera flatbread, eaten with a variety of stews, is a staple of Ethiopian cuisine.

ETHIOPIAN CUISINE AND DRINK

Cooking is a high art with a huge variety of dishes normally seen at their best at a wedding or special occasion. Most dishes are infused with *berbere*, a spice mixture containing very hot chili pepper. At home Ethiopians traditionally eat communally from one platter; they eat in a reserved way—it is considered impolite to stuff oneself—and, instead of cutlery, they use their right hand, which if used clumsily, should never be licked.

The staple grain is *teff*, which is made up into a large flatbread (*injera*) that covers a two-foot (sixty-centimeter) diameter plate. On this, various tasty stews (*wot*) and other dishes are piled. Guests sit around and help themselves to *injera*, which they wrap around the stews of their choice. At a less formal meal, the *injera* is cut up and served in rolls on a central platter, with each person taking a roll and helping themselves to the sauces, vegetables, and *wot* of their choice. Where *teff* is not plentiful, other grains may be used for the *injera*.

The *wot* is a cooked stew made out of meat, including chicken (*doro wot*), mutton (*ye beg wot*), and beef (*ye bere sega*). A commonly found dish is fried meat known as *tibs* (literally, "fried"). A stew without peppers is known as *alicha*—Ethiopians are usually conscious of the fact that many Westerners cannot take the heat of Ethiopian dishes, and so provide at least one or two of this type. *Kitfo* is very lightly cooked, or raw, minced meat. Cottage cheese (*ayb*) and various vegetables, including Ethiopia's own cabbage (*goman*), are added. Puddings are rare, although fresh fruit is handed around after a meal, but cakes are much appreciated, especially in coffeehouses.

On fasting days *misr wat* (lentils), *shiro wat*, made from ground chickpeas, and fish are allowed.

Honey is highly prized in Ethiopia, given to children as a sweet drink called *berz*, or an alcoholic wine known as *tej* for adults. *Talla* is the local beer, which is made from barley and flavored with an herb called *geisho*.

In Sidamo and Gurage the staple is a food made from *enset* (false banana); maize is grown and used in southern areas; and sorghum is used for making *injera* in those areas where *teff* cannot be grown. In the east, Somali foods, such as goat meat and rice, are more common.

Of all foreign influences on Ethiopian diet, the Italian has probably had the most impact. Pastas are well known everywhere, including in the most rural places. Introduced ingredients, such as the tomato, potato, and white cabbage, are well integrated into Ethiopian cooking.

EATING OUT AND BARS

Ethiopians love to eat out, and go to nightclubs and bars if young and unmarried. They prefer their traditional food, but there are many foreign dishes that, when spiced up, have been adapted to the Ethiopian taste. For example, the Ethiopian version of spaghetti bolognese

consists of a tomato sauce richly endowed with chili peppers or *berbere*. Ethiopian fish goulash is likely to be a spiced up, and drier, version of the Hungarian dish.

Most towns have a modern hotel where the more affluent Ethiopians might be found dining out; simple meals, such as an omelette (again spiced with chili peppers), are generally available in roadside restaurants. Since Ethiopians do not like to eat in public, chairs and tables in these establishments are usually well inside the building, or surrounded by a wall.

Being naturally curious people, educated Ethiopians are happy to join foreign friends for a meal at a hotel or restaurant of their choice; in Addis Ababa these may specialize in Indian, Armenian, Greek, or Italian cuisine, or any number of other cooking styles. Many of the same restaurants will also offer a spicy dish

Eating *tihlo*, a snack of barley dough balls dipped in stew.

to please their Ethiopian clientele. There are now American-style fast-food outlets in parts of Addis Ababa, and food delivery services. *Deliver Addis* is one such company that uses an online ordering system; when the driver arrives with the order he will telephone the customer, who comes out and pays him in cash.

Bars in cities and in the countryside are a common sight. Some bars favored by wealthy young Ethiopians and Westerners in Addis Ababa include "Black Pearl" near Edna Mall in the Bole area, "HQ Irish Pub' in "*Wollo Sefer*" nearby, and "Midtown Location" on the top floor of Boston Day Building in Bole Road.

Less respectable bars, which sometimes double up as brothels, are universally and euphemistically called *buna betoch* ("coffeehouses").

Drinking *tej* (honey mead) in a bar in Addis Ababa.

A *talla beit* ("beer house") is where local beer can be purchased in rural areas. Marked by an upturned mug or empty tin placed on top of a pole, they are functional and are not considered disreputable.

SPORTS

Ethiopians are passionate about sports; while they support team games, they excel at individual events such as running.

In middle-class Addis Ababa, tennis and cycling are popular sports. In villages, enthusiastic youngsters can be seen swiping a table tennis paddle at the public table. Any child, even in small villages, is likely to be familiar with English Premier League football teams. The soccer stadium in Addis Ababa is always full of loyal supporters for matches played there. However, Ethiopia as a nation has not achieved much success recently in this most popular of team games in Africa.

Running as an individual sport is much more successful, and Ethiopia regularly gains a formidable medal haul at the Olympic Games, especially in the 5,000 meter (3.1 miles), 10,000 meter (6.2 miles), and marathon events. Ethiopians are famous throughout the world for their long-distance running and are particularly noted for their "finishing kick," a ferocious finishing sprint. High-profile athletes such as Haile Gebreselassie, Kenenisa Bekele, and Tirunesh Dibaba are not only adored for their achievements, but also for their ability to raise Ethiopia's esteem as a nation.

Returning heroes are enthusiastically welcomed home as they step off the airplane, before being paraded down Bole Road. Groups of runners can be seen training on main roads or on the slopes of Entoto, the mountain behind Addis Ababa. The Great Ethiopian Run, a major annual charity event, attracts thousands of participants on a six-mile (ten-kilometer) run around Addis Ababa, which starts and finishes in Meskel Square, in the center of Addis Ababa.

In the countryside there are traditional games that are still played. *Gugs* is played on horseback, where two opposing horsemen rush at each other with lancelike poles and try to unseat the other. This remains popular in the Oromo districts around Addis Ababa.

Genna is a game similar to field hockey, where a ball is hit with sticks by players on opposing sides. This game is especially popular at Christmas, and indeed the name derives from the Amharic name for Christmas.

Being keen horsemen, Ethiopians have also adopted the Western games of polo, show jumping, and racing. In Oromia, weddings will include horsemen riding highly decorated mounts that they will proudly allow to be photographed.

MUSIC AND ART

There is a rich tradition of music, both popular and liturgical, with a number of instruments that reflect

Live music in Addis Ababa.

regional traditions. These include the *masinko*, a one-stringed instrument played with a bow; the *krar*, or lyre; and the *washint*, or pipe.

These instruments are often played by a singer, called an *azmari*. In a restaurant or nightclub, an *azmari* will make up impromptu songs, often to suit his audience, that are complimentary or insulting to the guests, or skillfully constructed to be both of these at once. This traditional wordplay, known as "wax and gold," is impossible to translate into English.

There is also a large following for bands and singers operating in the cities, using Western instruments such as saxophones. Many of these bands are influenced by traditional rhythms and folk music, but have developed them into a distinctive modern style that has an enthusiastic following among young Ethiopians, especially in the Jazz style. The Fendika Cultural Centre in Addis Ababa has a growing reputation with middle class Ethiopians and foreigners alike for music and the fine arts.

The traditional dance is called *eskista*, and consists largely of rolling the shoulders to the rhythm of the band.

Liturgical music dates back to a sixth-century Tigrayan, St. Yared. He is considered the father of Ethiopian Church music, inventor of the distinctive chant used in all Orthodox services, and creator of a notation system that predates the Western system. It is a matter of pride to be a member of one of the many church choirs that sing psalms and dance for services.

The visual arts are mainly based on the traditional form developed for ecclesiastical use, which is symbolic and two-dimensional in style; every church contains scenes from the Bible, and of the lives of the saints.

There is a growing appreciation among Ethiopians for abstract art practiced by artists who have mainly studied abroad, though there is a respected fine art school in Addis Ababa. Centers for the intellectual exploration of art in Ethiopia are appearing, such as the Zoma Museum, which aims to explore a fusion of Western with Ethiopian art forms. Some of the better-known galleries in Addis Ababa are the Alliance Française, the Makush Gallery, and St. George's Gallery. Many restaurants now hang work by modern Ethiopian artists, too.

Apart from religious devotional art that sells well, the visual arts (and humanities) are less highly valued than the sciences in the school curriculum.

SHOPPING

Almost anything you need can be bought somewhere in Addis Ababa—except perhaps very specialized goods, such as spare parts for certain vehicles, or artists' materials. Prices of particular goods vary enormously, from those charged in the Mercato market area to high prices at Western-standard supermarkets. Trawling the Mercato demands much stamina and an appreciation of bargaining techniques. It is just as cost-effective to shop at one of the many shopping arcades springing up all over town. Postcards and greeting cards are best bought at a good bookshop, a hotel shop, or the central post office. Ethiopian souvenirs are found in many kiosks behind the central post office and Churchill Avenue, or in big hotels. ATMs exist in the main hotels, at the main branches of the main banks, and at shopping malls, but not outside of town. Credit cards are becoming more commonly used, and are especially acceptable to the airlines and big travel agents. Despite these developments, and despite inroads made by local digital payment apps such as CBE Birr, Ethiopia is still mostly a cash-based society.

PLACES TO GO

In Addis Ababa, the extensive Gulele Botanic Garden on the slopes of Mount Entoto provides fresh air, walks, and views over the city. The new Unity Park, opened in 2019, was built around Menelik's palace and is an excellent example of modern museology: it combines a zoo, indigenous plants, vignettes of regional cultures, as well as the palace apartments, throne room, and banqueting halls. The history of the development of the Ethiopian state during the past 150 years can be followed here, and, in the basement of the throne room is a salutary exhibition devoted to the excesses of the Derg regime.

Also worth visiting are the National Museum, which houses the remains of the prehistoric hominid, Lucy, and provides a very good overview of paleontological discoveries; the Museum of the Institute of Ethiopian Studies, located at Haile

Blue Nile Falls, a popular attraction.

Selassie's palace in Addis Ababa University (AAU) with its fine collection of art and musical instruments; the Museum of Natural History, which is in the Science block of AAU; and the Addis Ababa Museum, in an old house on the south side of Meskel Square.

Outside town there are various scenic spots. You might take a half-day excursion up Mount Entoto, just north of Addis Ababa, where there are two historic churches, one of which is Entoto Mariam, precious to both Menelik and to Haile Selassie, with views both south across the city and north over the plains toward the Blue Nile headwaters. A day out to Bishoftu (Debre Zeit), along the Chinese-built expressway south of Addis Ababa, where there are a number of volcanic crater lakes, restaurants, and fruit juice bars, provides an antidote to Addis Ababa's polluted traffic jams.

Lake Langano, about 124 miles (200 kilometers) south of Addis Ababa, is the nearest Ethiopia has to a beach resort. It is now well equipped with hotels, lodges, and camping sites. The water is slightly alkaline and brown in color, but it is safe for swimming.

For a walk outside town, the Menagasha Suba forest (located west of Addis Ababa, and requiring a four-wheel drive vehicle), a circuit around the crater lake on the top of Mount Zukwala (near Bishoftu), or going down to the crater lake of Wonchi (near Ambo), are all day outings from Addis Ababa.

Of historical interest for a day out of Addis Ababa is one of the country's most southerly rock-hewn churches, at Adadi Mariam, two hours down the road to Butajira. The Debra Libanos Monastery associated with St. Tekle Haimanot, perched on the side of a gorge in the Blue Nile headwaters, is two hours north on the road to Bahr Dar.

Other main towns also have similar sites of historical and ecclesiastical interest suitable for a weekend away from Addis Ababa. Most have museums. For example, Mekele's main museum is sited in the former palace of Emperor Yohannes IV. In Jimma, the center of a former sultanate, the museum is devoted to the history of the sultans, and the newly restored Sultan Abba Jifar's palace on the edge of town is open to the public. In Harar, the museum focuses on ethnographic material of the Adari culture. The supposed house of the French poet Rimbaud is preserved, as are the old walls surrounding the town. Lalibela and Gondar are world famous for their respective rock-hewn churches and castles. Axum is famous for its centuries-old *stelae*, and for being the legendary repository of the original Ark of the Covenant.

There has recently been a huge growth of tourist accommodation, both luxurious and simple. Lodges have sprung up in some spectacular places, often using traditional designs in an innovative way. These include the Aregash Lodges among the coffee groves at Yirge Alem; the Ankober Palace Lodge, based on Menelik II's old palace, perched on the west scarp of the Rift Valley; and the Gheralta Lodge based near a cluster of rock-hewn churches in Tigray. Two luxury lodges are destinations in themselves: the Bale Mountain Lodge set above the Harenna Forest, and the Limalimo Lodge on the northern scarp of the Simien Mountains.

BEGGING

The giving of alms is embedded in Ethiopian culture. Well-to-do Ethiopians will always offer money to obviously infirm people, especially outside churches and mosques. Small change is often carried by Ethiopians for this purpose.

It is different for foreigners, whose indiscriminate benevolence can induce an avalanche of begging from the needy, and not so needy. Trained guides will usually advise against capitulating to these demands. It is wise to have a planned approach.

Depending on the history of the area and their exposure to foreigners, the local children's reaction to visitors ranges from a shy wave to supplication for sweets (*caramela*), or demands for money. On the whole, this can be resisted with politeness or humor. If necessary, a gift such as fruit or bread can be shared. A sympathetic *egziabher yistilign* "may God bless you" is often accepted by older people.

Many foreigners resort to giving to only a few beggars whom they see regularly and have gotten to know. There are also many charities, both Ethiopian and foreign, that provide a service to the needy in the streets and donating to these organizations is often a good approach. Bear in mind that there are other ways of helping enterprising Ethiopians, such as paying someone for looking after a car in the street.

TIPPING
....

In any place, at any time, for any reason, tips will be expected. Care and discernment, therefore, are needed if the unwary foreigner is not to be swamped by expectations.

Tipping in restaurants and cafés is reasonable. Only the more upscale restaurants levy a service charge, and customers will tip a few birr in addition to it—about 5 percent would be right. Tipping a shared line taxi or minibus driver is never done, although it would be expected if you hired a taxi for the day.

Small change is needed for many small favors. Generally speaking, if a small boy is appointed to look after your car the job will be carried out and he should be paid. Sometimes the amount might be queried and only experience will indicate what is fair, and whether you have the last word.

Often, tourist sites have their own methods of payment, security, and guides, and it is worth finding out what they are and keeping to the prevailing norm when tipping your guide. Not to do so invites corruption and an unfair inflation.

CHAPTER SEVEN

TRAVEL, HEALTH, & SAFETY

Ethiopia's transportation system and its health facilities are developing fast, but their full potential will not be realized for a few years. However, it is now possible to drive all the way to Gondar from Addis Ababa on an asphalt road, to enter an international standard hospital in Addis Ababa if you are sick, and stay in a five-star hotel. Although the general tourist infrastructure is not as good as in East Africa, the trade-off is that foreigners can experience more closely how Ethiopians live.

ETHIOPIANS ON THE MOVE

Ethiopians enjoy exploring their country if they can, and they also like to explore other countries, where they will be self-confident and independent-minded about finding their way. Within Ethiopia there are well-established trade routes that have been used for centuries. Moreover, Christian Ethiopians have long plied the Red Sea, or traveled overland, to make the pilgrimage to Jerusalem. The Queen of Sheba set the most famous precedent when she undertook her visit to King Solomon of Israel to assess his riches. As we have seen in Chapter 3, pilgrimages within Ethiopia are made by both Christians and Muslims to various holy places, involving journeys several days long, often on foot. In addition, diaspora Ethiopians travel to and from their adopted countries, and it is not unusual to hear Canadian and American accents, as well as German or Swedish, spoken by Ethiopians in the departure lounge at the airport.

ARRIVALS

Addis Ababa's Bole Airport is a major travel hub and connects dozens of cities throughout Ethiopia and wider Africa with the rest of the world. It is also the central hub of the country's main national carrier, Ethiopian Airlines. If you are staying in Ethiopia, visas are required, and are easily obtained online. They are also available on arrival to citizens of most Western countries. Renewal or extension of a visa can be made at the Immigration Office in the center of Addis Ababa.

Bole Airport is the usual entry point for foreigners, although some may arrive overland from Kenya, at Moyale, or from Sudan, at Metema, but visas on arrival are not available at these frontier posts.

The terminal at Bole was extended in 2019 and has many of the modern facilities expected of an international airport. However, most flights in and out are scheduled at roughly the same time in the evening, so it is likely to be crowded at that time and it is important to get into the right lines. Most officials speak good English and they will help you do this.

Your first important impression of Ethiopia is likely to be of its bureaucracy in process—usually efficient, but inordinately thorough. First, you need a visa (unless you have obtained one in advance online or from an Ethiopian embassy), for which you pay a fee in dollars or euros. These are available on arrival only to citizens of certain countries. You then pass through Immigration, where your passport will be stamped; check that your visa covers your intended stay, because there is always trouble if you inadvertently overstay your welcome. Lastly, you pass through Customs, which is usually straightforward.

At this point, unless there is someone waiting for you inside the terminal, you will leave the building on your own. Either hire a porter, who might be waiting just inside the building, or boldly push your cart through the barrier and over the road to the parking area on the other side, where your contact will likely be waiting amid the jostling crowd. You can also take a taxi from the car park.

Terminal 1 is for domestic and regional flights and is the old airport building, adjacent to the new one, which has fewer facilities than the international terminal. If for any reason your flight is delayed, there are well-stocked restaurants and coffee bars in the terminals. It is always useful to have small change in birr notes, for porters or to pay for airport parking.

Taxis from the airport are top of the range yellow taxis, which will take you anywhere. Establish your price in advance and do not allow your driver to augment this amount on any pretext.

TRANSPORTATION

Ethiopia has all forms of transport, much of it new. A new Chinese-built cross-border railway runs between the Lebu terminal in the southwest of Addis Ababa and Djibouti. It operates every other day, calling in at Adama and Dire Dawa. In Addis Ababa, the Chinese also built a light railway system, which traverses the city from east to west, with branch lines north to the Mercato and south to Kaliti. It is cheap but can be crowded during rush hour.

The national airline, Ethiopian Airlines, with a long and distinguished record, monopolizes most internal air travel, although it has been joined by some small commercial aircraft and helicopter businesses. There is also a private air ambulance service.

Air transport is a good way of traveling over Ethiopa's deeply dissected landscape and can take you to all the main tourist destinations and more, often leaving at the crack of dawn. Ethiopian Airlines domestic service has a two-tier pricing system, which is more expensive for nonresidents. A good discount is offered if you have taken an international flight with them. Helicopters are very expensive and have caused anger among local people for the insensitive way they are sometimes used. Regulating their landing places would remedy these complaints.

Luxury long-distance buses are cheaper than air travel and provide good services to all the main cities, although you do need to book them in advance. These buses are matched by even cheaper, less reliable, public buses. Public minibuses ply routes between towns and cities, sometimes direct, and sometimes necessitating changes at key towns. The cheap buses and minibuses usually depart from designated stations; minibuses only leave when they are full.

Within Addis Ababa there are blue minibuses known as *minibus*, which operate along fixed routes, advertised by a fare collector, who leans out of the window shouting the destination and collecting the

fares. These offer the best value for getting about town. Foreigners are not usually asked for more than the normal rate. The various local buses are often crowded, although very cheap, and locals will warn visitors about pickpockets.

GETTING ABOUT IN TAXIS

There are several grades of taxi. The most expensive is the private taxi that is colored yellow and is the only kind allowed to collect passengers at the airport in Addis Ababa. They will take you anywhere, and they can also be hired at all the main hotels. Fares should either be established in advance, or the meter used. Some drivers will claim their meter is not working in order to get a better price out of unsuspecting would-be passengers, in which case it is best to walk away and find another. Fares are usually more expensive at night.

There are also blue saloon cars, often Ladas, known as *taxis*, which will take you anywhere for a negotiated fare. However, although there are recognized fares for different journeys, the drivers will more than likely raise the amount for a susceptible foreigner. They are owned by private individuals or syndicates, and sometimes their roadworthiness shows all the signs of a veteran at the end of a long and honorable career. However, game for anything, they will take all your excess luggage, tied to the roof rack, if necessary. Their drivers will not always speak good English, and it is as well to have a written address or some idea of where

Lada taxis in the capital.

you are going if you intend to take a taxi to a private house. It is possible to hire these vehicles on a contract basis if you want a cheap and efficient way of making complicated journeys around town. If the experience with a driver is a good one, you can take his business card and use him regularly. One should be wary of taking one of these taxis late at night as the drivers at that time are not always in the best condition for responsible driving.

These taxis have been joined by a number of efficient minicab companies that operate ride-hailing apps, which are reliable and comfortable. RIDE is the most widely used, and cars can be ordered either through their app or by calling 8294. Others include PikPik and ZayRide. These apps are mostly designed to be used on Android rather than iPhone operating systems, as iPhones are not as commonly owned in Ethiopia. Any type of taxi is allowed to take you to the airport.

BAJAJ AND *GARI*

Outside Addis Ababa, taxis may not be so easy to find, but there is usually a plethora of *tuk tuks*, or *bajaj*, named for the Indian company that manufactures them. These can be flagged down in some surprising places, and on the steepest of hills. They will easily carry two people, and luggage in a hole behind the seat. *Garis*, pulled by rather emaciated looking horses, were once

very common. Introduced by the Italians during the 1936–41 occupation, these are still seen in provincial towns, but are now being replaced by *bajaj*.

RENTING CARS AND BOOKING FLIGHTS

Self-drive cars can be rented through travel agents, private individuals, or the usual international car rental companies. They are nearly always rented with a driver who will sometimes act as a guide. 4WD vehicles are not usually available without a driver. At the cheaper end of the market the car and driver offered to you may well turn out to be a privately-owned vehicle, rather than a company one, but they are not necessarily the worse for it. Payments can usually be made in Ethiopian birr, US dollars, or euros.

International or national driver's licenses are not recognized in Ethiopia. Foreign licenses have to be exchanged for local ones, but it is rarely worth a short-term visitor's time to wait in line for half a day to achieve this. If you have the time or need, you should go to an office of the Addis Ababa Road Transport Authority, where your national license will be deposited in return for an Ethiopian license. You should take passport photographs and money to pay for your license. When you leave the country you will need to retrieve your own national license. If you fail to do this, and there is a lapse of time before you renew your local license, your file will be found and you will have to pay retrospective fees.

FLIGHTS

Flights, both international and domestic, can be bought at any appropriate airline office or online. Ethiopian Airlines has a useable app for making bookings, and has offices in all the main towns. You can check in and book seats 24 hours before the flight. In Addis Ababa, the airline offices use a ticketed queuing system, and although this might involve a tedious wait, the staff are efficient once your turn comes. Cards are accepted.

ROADS

Western conventions for driving, such as keeping to the right of the road and making way for ambulances or pedestrians at crossings, are becoming more normal as the roads themselves improve. Improvements range from a Chinese-built express toll road between Addis Ababa and Adama, to new non-asphalt roads in rural areas, and new asphalting on existing roads. Some road building, once begun, seems to take time to finish, and the signs marking their destination remain aspirational. Meanwhile, clouds of dust and sudden barriers mark a road in progress.

Improved roads can very quickly develop potholes, slowing down traffic, and causing drivers to suspend the rule of right-hand driving. Night driving can also be hazardous when faced with broken-down vehicles or with faulty lights. Although using cell phones while driving is illegal, this rule is widely flouted.

Wry jokes are made about minibus drivers in Addis Ababa who are always in a hurry, but they display an extraordinary patience and skill in negotiating crowded roundabouts and congestion. The Shanghai Construction Group, which built overpasses in Addis Ababa, operates under the slogan, "Science, Cooperation, and Gumption." These are virtues needed to drive in contemporary Addis Ababa and it is not surprising that some foreigners choose in the end to employ a driver to get them about. Similarly, long-distance drivers of tourist minivans or 4WDs will need high levels of stamina when driving in Ethiopia.

Seat belts are obligatory for drivers, and when available, for passengers in the front. Third party insurance is mandatory. If an offense is committed, such as wrongful parking, police may remove your car's number plate, for redemption later. There are different speed limits for different roads which, when broken, incur fines that have to be paid the next day.

RULES OF THE ROAD

- Drive on the right
- The speed limit on open roads is 65 mph (110 kmph); in towns it is 25 mph (40 kmph)
- Seat belts are required nationally
- Cell phones may not be used while driving
- Priority is given to vehicles on traffic circles

In the past, pedestrians—who tended to walk on any part of the asphalt and to drive their animals on it—had an automatic right of way. Now the law has established that vehicles driving on fast, divided highways have priority (although not on the other roads) and it is unlawful for stock owners to haul animals over safety barriers in order to cross divided highways. Needless to say, the practice continues, and vigilance is still needed by drivers to avoid accidents.

Helpful road signs are being deployed in Addis Ababa, which indicate the way to different areas of the city, as well as directing traffic to the correct slip roads on the sometimes confusing dual carriageways. Many of these have few exit and entry points and sometimes it is necessary to drive a long distance past one's destination to get to a roundabout or slip road and double back. Street signs have also gone up in the center of town and on the main roads, which are less useful because although the names also appear on modern street maps, local people do not know the names. They mostly continue to use local reference points, such as a church, embassy, or hotel.

Outside the towns, few people have access to cars, and their main form of transportation is likely to be a horse or donkey, or their feet. Crowds of people all walking in one direction toward a village usually denote market day in that place. However, ever entrepreneurial locals have mobilized aged Land Rovers and trucks to link remote communities, and there is a surprisingly good system of buses on other rural roads.

Gasoline (*benzene*) and diesel (*naphta*) are imported, mostly from Sudan, through Metema and Gondar, although some comes from Djibouti. Supplies can run out without apparent reason, and no travel to remote places should be undertaken without taking spare jerricans of fuel and water.

WALKING IN CITIES

Walking is usually safe enough, although pollution and traffic in Addis Ababa might make it unpleasant to do so. A walk on Mount Entoto or in the Botanic Garden at Gulele provides clean air and good views, even if the altitude may prove exhausting.

The sight of foreigners walking anywhere in the sun is unusual and can attract the attention of crowds of children, although this problem is improving. They can either be ignored, or turned to advantage, by appointing one as a guide, setting a fee in advance, and instructing him (usually a male) to keep the others at bay. However, like any city, there are areas frequented by pickpockets, areas where foreigners are not particularly welcome, and times of day when it is unwise to be about. The opulent area of Bole, near the airport, is becoming one such area. Take advice from locals if you are unsure of the safety of an area.

If you are seen walking any distance you may well attract the attention of curious Ethiopians wanting to practice their English. However, pure altruism is rare and, inevitably, the youth may well try to push his advantage and obtain something from you, whether information about US green cards, an address, or try to offer a bogus discount.

WHERE TO STAY

There is a good choice of hotels in Addis Ababa. They range from international standard hotels, often with swimming pools, to humbler guesthouses mostly in the Bole Road and Churchill Road areas. There is also a good choice of accommodation on booking.com and Airbnb. The bigger hotels all act as hubs for expatriate social life; they also have travel agents and souvenir

A lodge-style hotel near Lake Tana.

shops operating inside them. There is good public transportation from any of these hotels.

Outside Addis Ababa there are adequate hotels in all the main towns, although electricity and plumbing might not be as promised. Tourist accommodation has improved greatly in choice and comfort, and some owners have made special efforts to build in an architectural style in keeping with the area.

For anyone planning on staying for some time, houses or apartments can be rented through an agent, or by recommendation. Agents can also be found by word of mouth, and there are notice boards at the big hotels and supermarkets serving affluent areas that advertise accommodation, cars, or sales by expatriates leaving the country. Renting a house will certainly involve a contract with payment in advance for several months.

HEALTH

Keeping Clean and Taking Precautions

Ethiopia has no fewer germs than anywhere else, a fact well-known by the locals, who will always bring you a basin of water, soap, and a towel, or show you to a tap to wash your hands before eating. The tap water is cleaner than in most African countries, but it is still advisable to wash all vegetables and fruit in a germicide, and to filter drinking water. Locally bottled water is found everywhere and any café will stock it, although there are now issues about the amount of plastic this generates. During the dry months, when reservoirs are low, tap water may not be available, but warning is usually given and it is a good idea to keep some jerricans full of water during those times.

Clinics and Hospitals

There are any number of public and private clinics in Addis Ababa and other main towns. Doctors rely on their private practices to make ends meet. Foreigners usually attend private clinics if their embassies do not have a clinic of their own to service their own communities. Ethiopian doctors often hold private clinics in their area of specialization and, to some extent, you do your own diagnosis, and then find the right doctor. Ethiopian doctors are highly competent, and tend to be among the intellectual elite, but there are not enough of them. There are a number of very good private hospitals in Addis Ababa, such as the Landmark Hospital, the Korean Christian Hospital, St. Gabriel's, and the Brass Maternity Hospital. If you break an arm, for example, every part of the diagnosis and treatment will need to be paid for separately. It should be said, however, that Ethiopians tend not to attend clinics and hospitals unless their symptoms are well advanced, and the line in which you are waiting may contain people who are much worse off than you.

Most Ethiopians will also hedge their bets and use traditional healers or medicine. Tapeworm is a very common complaint, and the usual cure for this is a concoction of the toxic flowers of the *kosso* tree (*Hagenia abyssinica*).

HIV/AIDS

While great inroads have been made in the fight against HIV/AIDS in Ethiopia, it still exists in many parts of the country, particularly along truck drivers' routes, in brothels, and in garrison towns. In 2018, the overall incidence among adults was reduced to an estimated 1 percent of the population, which represents a remarkable improvement compared to just a decade ago when that figure stood at 5 percent. AIDS related deaths have also halved in that time. Ethiopia's public campaign about AIDS/HIV is relatively open, but when a person dies of AIDS, the cause is not usually openly stated, and it would be grossly insensitive to suggest it was so. AIDS tests can be had in most clinics.

LATRINES

These are not a strong point in Ethiopia. In general, men do not hesitate to use ditches and fences when the need arises, and there are certain unallocated areas in Addis Ababa where a close eye is needed on the ground when walking. The situation is so elemental that even citizens from neighboring countries will draw attention to this particular shortcoming.

Indoors, the facilities are sometimes no better, especially in country hotels where the plumbing breaks down and water might be intermittent. Latrines are either seats or, more likely, a "squat" that can be hard on creaky knees. The plumbing is based on the small-bore Italian system that is easily blocked if paper and sundries are flushed down the pipes. Toilet paper should always be taken as none will be found in public places outside Addis Ababa. However, in reputable restaurants or hotels in the main cities, there is no cause for complaint.

SECURITY

It is as well to remember that in African cities people tend to watch the world go by and they will remember you, even when you may have hardly noticed them. Most of them will be friendly or benign, but one or two will be looking out for an opportunity, such as catching you after you have withdrawn money at an ATM.

Muggings and thefts are not common, but they do happen, and visitors should take sensible precautions. Keep the number of valuables you carry with you to a minimum (including expensive jewelry and watches), do not count banknotes openly, keep your hand firmly on your bag, and where possible, walk with a companion.

The Mercato, Bole, and Piazza areas of Addis Ababa seem to attract pickpockets. Every house and public building has *zebagnias* (guards), who are sometimes armed. To enter major public buildings, such as the Central Bank, big hotels, or museums, an X-ray or body search is required. Addis Ababa also teems with a variety of people, some of whom come from countries at odds with Ethiopia's interests, and lethal bombs have been planted in the past in public places and in taxis—Ethiopians themselves are well aware of this particular danger. Foreigners are advised to only take reliable taxis home in the late hours.

In some rural areas young boys find it good fun to lob stones at foreigners. Lobbing stones toward animals that they are tending is often done to attract their attention or to divert them, and the boys can be very good shots. However, this display of bad manners warrants a vigorous verbal response, or a judicious hasty withdrawal.

There are parts of the country where it is most unwise to go for pleasure: south of Jijiga, in the Ogaden, foreigners run the risk of kidnap or ambush; they are very unlikely to be allowed anywhere near the frontier with Eritrea while the situation remains hostile.

Elsewhere is generally safe, including the Danakil Depression; but, if on a private tour with one's own car, it is essential to ask for local advice in case there are local tensions or particular places where foreigners are unwelcome. The desert area of the Danakil, in any event, should never be entered unless you have adequate water and preferably a local guide. The hottest annual mean temperature on Earth was recorded there, at Dallol—94° F (34° C).

In general terms, if you are traveling privately by car, you should check where you are likely to be able to obtain fuel—sometimes it runs out without warning— and take spare jerricans. Spare tires, including a second spare and a repair kit, should also be taken, although *gomistas* (puncture repair shops) are numerous along the main routes. Breakdowns can sometimes be remedied by an innovative mechanic or a passing truck driver but, again, this tends to be on the main routes only.

Valuables

It is not really necessary to travel with valuables in Ethiopia, unless they are electronic ones. Ethiopians themselves dislike ostentation, and it is bad manners to draw attention to opulence in a place where most people so obviously cannot obtain the same material goods. However, in Addis Ababa most middle-class and wealthy families will acquire the same gadgets as their counterparts in the West, perhaps more. Valuables should be carefully looked after, or locked away, when not in use, because there are plenty of people who would seize the opportunity to take what they can, even if they have no use for them. Most Ethiopians would be deeply embarrassed if this happened to their foreign friends.

Scams

Ethiopians are sometimes adept at trapping visitors in situations where they will feel a moral obligation to pay a lot of money for a service they would rather not have used, or for an article they would rather not have bought. For example, you can be invited to a coffee ceremony, or to see some cultural dancing, then taken on a long journey to a private house, on the pretext you are all great friends; after the briefest of cups of coffee, you will be asked a quite outrageous fee. Or you might be persuaded to accept a discount for a high-end product such as a hired car, only to find it is a public taxi.

Do not go on long journeys by car with strangers to unknown parts of the city. Try to avoid engaging with unofficial guides around the main tourist hotels. Remember that changing money unofficially can get you into trouble, resulting, at the very least, in the confiscation of your money; for an Ethiopian it would be imprisonment.

CHAPTER EIGHT

BUSINESS BRIEFING

THE BUSINESS ENVIRONMENT

Ethiopian businesses operate within different cultures: there are, on the one hand, the traditional businesses based on age-old trading of goods and services around the country and across the Red Sea; and others that owe their origins to family businesses set up in the twentieth century, often by Yemenis, Greeks, Armenians, and Italians. Nowadays, modern businesses can be branches of global enterprises, and diaspora Ethiopians are as likely to be investors as Chinese and Europeans. The nature of business has also expanded to include service industries such as advertising and consulting.

Business growth has been fostered within the framework of "developmental state" policy—a form of state-guided capitalism in which the state has kept control of the national airlines, electricity, and telecommunications utilities. But the principle of state control over aspects of the economy is being eroded in the face of Forex shortages.

Traditional trading is dominated by Muslims with connections to other Muslim countries in the region and involves goods that most westerners are hardly aware of: *Chat* is exported to Somalia, lentils to Sudan, and cattle to Saudi Arabia; in the other direction, there are imports through city hubs, such as Dire Dawa and Jijiga, of white goods and clothing. Gurage people also have a reputation as adept businessmen and can be found running anything from street kiosks to supermarket chains. Markets exist in all large towns, and weekly markets in smaller places, many of which are centuries old.

The privatization of many sectors nationalized by the Derg is part of an ongoing policy to attract foreign investment and expand business. Many previously state-owned hotel chains are now in private hands and have been joined by new boutique hotels as well as international chains. Floriculture, construction, textiles, and tourism were among the first sectors to attract foreign investment, including from diaspora Ethiopians. The success of "developmental state" policies is seen in the double-figure percentage annual growth of the economy since 2000.

Women entrepreneurs are now making considerable inroads into what was once a male-dominated sector often in fashion-related businesses, such as leather and textiles.

Ethiopia's principal exports are coffee, leather, sesame seed, and other grains and pulses, and, more recently, cut flowers. *Chat* is also a major informal export commodity. Foreign exchange is also earned through the provision of services to Addis Ababa's vast diplomatic community, based around the headquarters of the United Nations Economic Commission for Africa and the African Union. Ethiopian Airlines is a rapidly expanding and highly profitable state-owned company, providing training services to other airlines, and Bole Airport is a hub for Africa. Tourism is growing and there will soon be exports of hydroelectric power. Nonetheless, the value of imports greatly exceeds that of exports.

Parastatal monopolies, dating back to Imperial and Marxist days, and now referred to as state-owned enterprises, are often more efficient than you might expect. Ethiopian Airlines and the electricity utility are among the front-runners. By contrast, Ethio Telecom, Ethiopian Shipping Lines, various state-owned banks, and the Addis Ababa Water Authority attract more criticism, but provide an adequate if not sparkling service. Ethio Telecom's stranglehold on Internet services, which are very poor and expensive, provokes widespread resentment.

There are also a number of companies owned by endowment funds linked to political parties. These companies have investments in textiles, engineering, import and export of coffee and grains, drip irrigation, pharmaceuticals, and much else besides. There are sometimes complaints these companies enjoy favored status in access to bank loans, and to government contracts, but they are not necessarily immune from prosecution if they break the law.

Chinese investment in recent years has been very significant and includes the manufacture of construction materials, pharmaceuticals, and much else.

Banks, many of which are now building headquarters in the National Theatre area of central Addis Ababa, often have loose and unacknowledged connections to regional states or to particular Ethiopian nationalities: Nib International Bank is Gurage-focused; Wagagen Bank is more Tigray-oriented; and there are three banks linked with the development of Oromia.

Businesses and government offices tend to be open Monday through Friday from 8:30 a.m. to 5:30 p.m., with a lunch break of up to an hour. This break starts at 11:30 a.m. on Fridays to allow Muslim employees to attend midday prayers at the mosque. Retail businesses, and most banks, are also open on Saturday mornings.

INVESTING IN ETHIOPIA

Foreign investment in the Ethiopian economy is encouraged by the Ethiopian Investment Commission.

It is relatively easy to set up an enterprise, either as a wholly foreign-owned company or as a joint venture. An initial investment will need to be made in foreign exchange and deposited in a bank. This will enable you to open an office and apply for work permits for any foreign staff. Representative offices of foreign companies may be set up on payment of a substantial deposit in foreign exchange, but they are not allowed to trade.

Foreign business representatives will find it worth contacting any one of a number of efficient "business incubators" in Addis Ababa, or by contacting the European Business Forum in Ethiopia or the American

Chamber of Commerce in Ethiopia. The Ethiopian Investment Commission on Bole Road, Addis Ababa, provides an investors' one-stop-service for work permits, residence permits, trade licenses, and company registrations.

If you seek to do business in Ethiopia, and accept the constraints of the culture, you can make good profits. The Ethiopians will hope that you retain those profits, at least in part, inside the country. If you are ready to become a member of the Ethiopian business community, you will be welcomed.

Bole in Addis Ababa.

INVESTMENT: A QUICK GUIDE

Although regulations change from time to time, here are some broad guiding principles:

- Investment in certain sectors such as weapons manufacture, international air transport, electricity generation, and postal services (not courier), can only be made jointly with the government
- Banking, insurance, and the export of coffee, among other sectors, are reserved only for Domestic investors
- Joint investment is allowed between Domestic and Foreign investors in such areas as domestic air transport, public relations, films, and accountancy
- The foreign share of a joint Foreign-Domestic investment is limited to not more than 75 percent in some cases, or to not more than 49 percent in others
- Investors need to submit their papers with the Ethiopian Investment Commission. Administration for setting up a representative's office is done through the Ministry of Trade
- A minimum of US $200,000 is required for a wholly foreign-owned investment (less for some consultancy services) and US $150,000 for a joint venture with an Ethiopian

THE BUSINESS CULTURE

Ethiopian businesspeople are said to have an aversion to risk. This is understandable; they have plenty of risks to be averse to. Over the years some of the country's most prominent entrepreneurs and business executives have spent months or even years behind bars, accused of corruption offenses for which they have never formally been charged, or for which they have been finally and belatedly exonerated. Influence and power within organizations such as the Chambers of Commerce and the Confederation of Ethiopian Labor Unions (CELU) are often subject to political forces that foreigners do not understand.

The tendency to mistrust and question people's motives, which underlies so much of Ethiopian culture, is prominent in business culture, too. There is a fear that contracts will be unenforced, that promises will not be kept. As a consequence, many transactions are in cash; personal or company checks are not commonly accepted, and when used will generally be cashed within an hour or two of receipt. People tend to prefer to do business with old and trusted associates, or at the very least to spend time building a relationship with a new acquaintance, before they will go very far in negotiating a contract.

In practice, a business relationship may begin with an introduction, followed by a meeting in a coffee shop—on neutral territory. This may last up to an hour. Then, if it is established that business of mutual benefit is at least possible, an invitation to

an office or production facility will be suggested.
Lunch may be taken at a local restaurant, and
slowly and very politely a visiting businessperson
will be assessed. Ethiopians are often extremely
shrewd judges of character; if they think you are
straightforward and have integrity, you can look
forward to a long and rewarding association. If not,
you will be politely dropped.

You may have the misfortune to meet altogether
dodgier characters if you have no introduction to
mainstream business networks. These types scout
for investment partners from overseas, hoping to
secure very large cash investments in return for a
very small shareholding. They often claim access
to, or influence with, regional authorities, or to vast
tracts of agricultural land. Be wary of anyone seeking
to push you into a quick contract; and refrain from
making even a verbal agreement that you will be held
to. Honest agreements in Ethiopia are nearly always
carefully thought through and are almost invariably
in writing.

Direct corruption or bribery in Ethiopia is on the
increase, although traditional values predominate,
and the type of rampant corruption seen in some
countries is generally frowned upon. If it occurs
in a business transaction, and is discovered, the
legal penalties can be severe. More subtle forms
of corruption, such as under-invoicing or over-
invoicing, can also lead a foreigner into deep waters.
Much more common is the asking of a favor once
a deal has been done. This may be anything from

the purchase of a laptop computer, to the provision of fees to a second cousin for higher education in Canada or Australia. Similarly, a request for assistance in obtaining a visa for a relative to a European country or to North America, by providing a letter of invitation, for example, is not uncommon.

LEGALITIES

The civil and commercial codes of Ethiopia are available in print in English, and are a useful resource. Companies, which may be either Share Companies or Private Limited Companies, are easy enough to form and register. They are regulated by the federal and regional ministries of Trade and Industry, in accordance with the provisions of the Ethiopian Commercial Code. No business may operate without a trade license, which has to be renewed annually.

It is important to get employment contracts carefully written and signed; otherwise difficulties will arise with your workforce at a later date. This can lead to court actions, which are common. Contribution to a national insurance scheme is mandatory unless a private one is in use; both the employer and the state pay into it. There are also other obligations to employees such as holiday entitlement and employment security.

The legal process is slow in Ethiopia, which tends to make contracts unenforceable in practice, if not in theory. This can lead to late payment and other difficulties. It is as well, therefore, to include in any contract some agreement to arbitration, short of recourse to the courts. It is wise to develop a relationship of trust with Ethiopian colleagues, but at the same time to write contracts clearly and carefully.

EXCHANGE CONTROL

The Ethiopian currency is called the birr, divided into 100 centimes, known in Amharic as *santim*.

In 2020 the value of the birr was approximately 30 to the US dollar. The birr has depreciated against the dollar over the years. Its value against all other currencies depends on the current value of the US dollar. Although investors are allowed to maintain accounts in hard currencies, exchange control regulations are quite complex and are strictly enforced. At times of foreign exchange shortage, it may take weeks or months to open a letter of credit, or to repatriate dividends.

There is also a parallel market for foreign exchange, in cash, operating illegally. Many people use this market, but it is not for the inexperienced, and if caught, prosecution can follow.

BUREAUCRACY

Ethiopian bureaucracy is extremely efficient, if often slow and complex. You will encounter it if you need a driver's license, insurance coverage, a bank account, or a residence permit.

File keeping is meticulous and officials of all ranks are generally helpful if you adopt a patient and humble approach. Any operation, from cashing a check in a bank to renewing a driver's license, will involve half a dozen people handling your request, issuing invoices and receipts, and processing and receiving money. All will do their work methodically, and you will generally come away with your business completed relatively quickly, unless you have the misfortune to hit a tea or lunch break, a staff meeting, or a training day. In this case nothing will happen until everyone gets back to their desks.

MEETINGS

Dress

You may be surprised to see that only the most senior people in a ministry or a commercial company will be very smartly dressed. However, if you are going to meet someone at the top of an enterprise, you should be prepared to be smartly dressed yourself. For men, this means a suit and a tie, and neatly polished shoes; for women a greater variety is possible and trousers may be worn, dressed up or down as appropriate. In the countryside, Western formality hardly exists in business meetings. No one will be so impolite as to draw attention to shortcomings in anyone's attire.

Etiquette

Ethiopians are a polite people and will always rise to greet a visitor to their office. They will shake hands, and invite you to take a seat, before they attend to your business. They will generally address you by your title (Mr., Mrs., Dr., Reverend, or whatever), in conjunction with your first name, rather than your surname, and will expect the same from you. Government ministers and senior businessmen will certainly expect to be called *Ato* (Mr.), *Woizero* (Mrs.), or *Woizerit* (Miss), and if they have a doctorate to be addressed as Doctor. For ambassadors and ministers the use of "Your Excellency" is appropriate. Orthodox and Catholic Bishops are "Your Beatitude," and the Orthodox Patriarch is "Your Holiness."

It is conventional in Ethiopia to open the conversation with an exchange of polite questions along the lines of "How are you, are you well?" followed by inquiries about your family. Once this dialogue is concluded, you can get down to discussion of the main subject of your meeting. It is important not to skip the preliminaries and not to interrupt.

Making Your Case

Ethiopian businesspeople will respond well to an articulate, clearly reasoned, verbal presentation of your proposal. Technical presentations from a laptop computer may also be of help. People will listen attentively until you have finished, and then respond. You may then converse and exchange views until both parties feel they are of one mind. When presented with a challenge, Ethiopians can display enormous enthusiasm and innovation in the finding of a solution. They will not hesitate to explain politely why your own ideas might be wrong and to suggest another course of action. If you are the person to whom a proposal is being presented, bear in mind that you are not expected to interrupt during the initial presentation, but to save your questions until later.

Negotiations

If a discussion concerns a price, you may have to compromise and bargain, so you might as well start by asking for somewhat more than you expect to receive. The tone should be polite and never confrontational.

Don't expect decisions to be made on the spot. These are often made behind the scenes and you may be asked back several times before receiving a reply.

Disagreements should never involve raised voices. You may find at the end of a meeting that your point has been taken silently, if not overtly. Try to find ways to compromise, even at the cost of delay. Remember that Ethiopians are extremely patient, and that they always believe that time is on their side. You may be the one who is leaving on an airplane early the next morning, and you will be at a disadvantage. Don't be afraid to use delaying tactics yourself.

CONTRACTS AND FULFILLMENT

Should disagreement arise over fulfillment of a
contract it is as well to remember that litigation is
an Ethiopian national sport. It is very hard to do
anything in Ethiopia without an occasional brush
with the courts, since anybody who is aggrieved will
bring a civil action as a first rather than a last resort.

It is normally wise to seek a settlement out of
court, which is easy enough to do, through the
traditional system of adjudication by "elders."
Each party appoints two or three "elders," or
representatives, who need not be old, but should at
least hold a position in society, who will meet and
recommend a settlement. If that is acceptable, the
court case is withdrawn.

If an out of court settlement cannot be reached,
legal process and appeals to higher courts can take
several years to conclude.

WOMEN ENTREPRENEURS

The rise of many women to the top in business, law,
and politics is a feature of modern Ethiopia. They will
expect to be treated by men as equals, and if they are
in senior positions they are likely to be both tough
and decisive. They have been helped on their way,
despite the constrictions of traditional culture, by
the passion of Ethiopians for modernity. They have
also been helped by the presence in Addis Ababa of

President Sahle-Work Zewde, right, greets Ms. Arancha González of the International Trade Center, 2018.

a vast array of international organizations, which have brought contemporary standards of equal employment to the country. Women with power and influence are now a permanent feature of the Ethiopian scene.

CHAPTER NINE

COMMUNICATING

LANGUAGE

The official language of the federal Ethiopian government is Amharic, or *Amarinya*, a member of the South Semitic language family. It is widely used as a lingua franca, is the official language of Addis Ababa, and of several Southern and Western regional states, and was once universally taught in schools as the national language. Amharic is a grammatically complex and subtle language, and is hard for outsiders to learn really well, but the effort to learn just a few words will be useful and widely appreciated.

Amharic is written in Ge'ez script, derived from an ancient South Arabian alphabet. It is written from left to right and each letter represents a syllable, consisting of a basic consonant with a vowel added to it. There are more than 224 possible written letters, made up by multiplying each of thirty-two consonants by seven variants, denoting the following vowel sound. The total number varies slightly depending on which of Ethiopia's Semitic languages the alphabet is used for. One of Ethiopia's grand traditions is the priest's school in which small children learn these letters—so if you pass through a churchyard, and hear children chanting "*Ha Hu Hi Ha He Huh Ho*," they are hard at work on the alphabet, or *fidel*.

Learning Amharic

If you are staying long-term in Ethiopia and would like to make a serious attempt to master the language, including the alphabet, it is probably best to combine formal classes in grammar with informal conversation, and a great deal of rote learning. There are numerous agencies providing classes in Amharic, and any number of private tutors. Courses are widely available, especially through the seminary of the Mekane Yesus Church, and the Italian Cultural Institute. There are a number of phrase books available in bookshops, and audio courses are available too.

A FEW HANDY WORDS

If you are less ambitious linguistically, but would still like to have a few words, buy a phrase book and ask for help from those you meet. Here are some words to get you started:

Awon, or *Ow* – yes

Ai – no

Alla – there is

Yelem – there isn't

Ishi – OK

Ebakeh (male), *Ebakesh* (female), *Ebakwo* (polite) – please

Amesegenalehu or *Egziabher istilign* – thank you

Tenayistilign – hello

Indimin neh (male), *Indimin nesh* (female), *Indimin not* (polite) – how are you?

Dehna, Egziabher Yimesgen – well, thanks be to God

At first sight the basic greetings, and the words for "thank you" and "please," appear something of a mouthful, but you will soon get the hang of them. Be aware that different forms are used when addressing males or females, or persons to whom you wish to show respect.

Other Languages

Other regional languages in official use include Afan
Oromo used in Oromia; Somali, in Somali Region;
Afar in Afar Region, Tigrinya in Tigray; and Adare,
spoken in Harar. Many of these languages are now
written in a Latin script, which occasionally gives
unexpected values to familiar letters. Thus, a hotel
in Somali is *Xooteel*, where "x" represents the "h"
sound; and *Maxamed* represents the common name
Mohammed. In Afan Oromo, however, "x" represents
a voiced "t" sound, and "q" a voiced "k" sound, both
consonants having a sort of "click" sound.

Geʾez is an ancient language, no longer spoken but
still used as the liturgical language of the Orthodox
Church. Its closest modern descendant is Tigrinya,
spoken in Tigray and Eritrea. Amharic and Gurage
also derive from Geʾez.

Foreign Languages

English is the most widely used foreign language.
Many Ethiopians speak it fluently, particularly
educated people from before the time of the Derg,
and, of course, those who have been brought up
abroad. An Ethiopian educated within the country
will speak thoughtfully, deliberately, and often softly,
and the accent will be similar to English spoken in
the Middle East.

Because English has been the medium of
education for so long, certain particularly Ethiopian
English idioms have acquired currency in the
country. "Are you fine?" will be commonly used

in place of "Are you well?" If you knock on a door, you may well hear the response "Get in," rather than "Come in."

Ethiopians, with their connections to the diaspora in North America and Europe, are now likely to speak a range of languages other than their own or English. Older people who had connections with the former Italian colony of Eritrea, or who remember the occupation of 1936–41, may understand basic Italian. Many Italian words have also entered the Amharic language, for example *macchina* (car), or *mercato* (market). There is also an Italian community school from which Ethiopians have graduated.

In the southeast, close to the former French colony of Djibouti and alongside the original Djibouti–Addis Ababa French-built railway, many people know French, and you can safely say *au revoir* in Harar and people will understand.

The French Lycée Guebre Mariam in Addis Ababa has educated very many Ethiopians alongside Francophone expatriates, adding French to the several languages Ethiopians might speak. Its influence is reinforced by the thriving French cultural center, the Alliance Française, which has a strong interest in historical and archaeological studies. French words that have entered Amharic include *la gare* (railway station).

There are also words of Greek origin in Amharic, such as *terapeza* (table) and *pappas* (bishop), which were introduced long ago.

The foreign language that has had the longest association with Ethiopia is Arabic. Many traders use this language, especially those of Yemeni or Saudi origin. Very many words are common, or similar, to both Arabic and Amharic—for example, *faras* (horse), *muz* (bananas), and *birtukan* (oranges, or "Portugal fruit").

FORMS OF ADDRESS AND BODY LANGUAGE

When addressing someone, on the telephone or in the flesh, whether in English or Amharic, it is polite to use *Ato* (Mr.), *Woizero* (Mrs.), *Woizerit* (Miss), followed by that person's first name. So, Ethiopia's current Prime Minister, Dr. Abiy Ahmed, would be addressed as *Dr. Abiy*, not *Dr. Ahmed*. Ahmed is the Prime Minister's father's given name.

Ethiopians go through life with their personal or given name, followed by their father's first name. Sometimes, they may also add their paternal grandfather's name if there is likely to be confusion. Married women never take their husband's name.

When greeting a person in the flesh, it is normal to bow slightly while you shake hands. A person who feels greatly subservient will offer a wrist, not a hand. If you are seated, you should make at least a halfhearted attempt to rise to your feet to greet a newcomer. The person entering the room will almost certainly protest politely before you reach the standing position.

In Amharic it is conventional to ask several times how you are. Replies should be positive and affirmative; bad news can be saved for further into the discussion. This occasionally comes into English as "How are you? Are you fine? Fine, thanks be to God." Close friends of the same sex, or the opposite sex, may kiss each other three or four times on both cheeks on meeting after a period apart. Warm greetings also take the form of touching opposite shoulders as you shake hands.

Ethiopians can be tactile. If you see two traffic policemen holding hands, it does not mean they are gay, merely close friends. The sight of couples holding hands is increasingly common in the city, but is still considered a bit "forward."

It is normal in Ethiopia to stand somewhat closer to another person when waiting in line for a bus than you would in the West. Nevertheless, bumping into another person in the street is not polite, and you should always say *yikirta* (excuse me) if this happens.

GOOD MANNERS, RETICENCE, AND SOCIAL NUANCES

After the initial greetings and mutual expressions of interest in the health of the other, it is usual to be somewhat circumspect in one's inquiries. It would be considered impolite to go straight into one's own agenda, not to say unwise, for it is more productive to explore obliquely the agenda of the other before putting your case.

Ethiopians rarely raise their voice in anger with others. Foreigners who do this invite either a sullen response, because Ethiopians hate to be shamed in front of other people, or the derision reserved for those who lack self-control.

On meeting a group of people, it is polite to acknowledge all of them, including the driver or maid, with a handshake. On entering a house, any domestic helpers present should be acknowledged when you meet your host. Both upon greeting and during a conversation, eye contact is important and should be maintained as far as is comfortable.

In general conversation Ethiopians tend to be reticent about their personal circumstances, a habit born of generations of experience of living under authoritarian regimes, and in a competitive atmosphere where jobs are hard to come by. Family information, personal tragedies and the like, are unlikely to be volunteered. Some imagination is needed, therefore, on the basis of age, region, and politics, to guess someone's personal history and to be sensitive. Many families have lost a member through war, or during the Derg regime, or have relatives in exile or who are economic migrants.

When inviting Ethiopians from diverse walks of life to one party, great care should be taken in bringing them together. The factors that might divide one Ethiopian from another are not just based on region; there are also class and ideological differences that are as subtle as the British class system. Do not assume, for example, that a prominent Tigrayan will enjoy the company of a prominent Oromo at your dinner table. Political passions and loyalties run very deep. Nor should you expect a well-qualified young person to be a good leader in a society where great respect is given to older people.

Always ask permission if you take a photograph of a person who you do not know, you could find yourself at the sharp end of a business negotiation: either respect people's privacy and ask before taking a photograph, or expect to pay something if you do.

HUMOR

Ethiopians have a good sense of humor beneath their rather sober and self-controlled exterior. They

thoroughly enjoy banter using wit and puns. At a more basic level they have a good sense of fun which becomes more noticeable when political tensions ease. They also love slapstick and, while they might sympathize, they would still laugh at a friend's misfortune, say, if he fell off a horse. They would not be so rude as to laugh at a stranger's misfortune, and they would be deeply sympathetic if the misfortune were illness or financial.

Ethiopian humor comes out in using odd names for common things. The special yellow taxis that go only to the airport are called "President," because Ethiopia's mainly ceremonial heads of state are thought to spend their days going to and from the airport to meet foreign dignitaries; rural trucks overloaded with people are called "Al Qaeda" because of the sometimes deadly crashes they cause.

THE MEDIA

The government radio broadcasts in several local languages, as well as in English, and there are now private stations broadcasting in Amharic and other languages. There are many current affairs programs, phone-in programs, news bulletins, and music programs.

The television has two channels, both run by government-owned Ethiopian Television. Those who have access to satellite television, including many bars and hotels, will also watch CNN, BBC World, and

numerous sports channels. It is quite normal to leave the television on during a meal at home, and for it to be on in the background in hotels and restaurants.

Newspapers are generally in English, Amharic, or Afan Oromo. The best-known English tabloid weeklies are *Capital*, *Fortune*, and *The Reporter*, all available online. The government publishes the *Ethiopian Herald* as a broadsheet, and there are increasing numbers of magazines available, some lasting only for one or two issues. Boys in the street will often sell *Time*, *Newsweek*, or *The Economist* to people sitting in their cars at traffic lights. These may be recycled copies. There are surprisingly few other foreign newspapers.

The press mainly operates on the principle of intelligent self-censorship. If any newspaper goes too far in criticism of government policy, or of powerful personalities, it may be closed down, and the editor arrested. This does not mean that the papers are not free to disagree politely with official policy, but it does mean that there is little deep investigative journalism, and that if criticism is made it is often by oblique means. A speech from an opposition figure may be printed in full, alongside a forthright condemnation by the editor of the opinions expressed. This way it will have been printed, without risk of condemnation.

TELEPHONES AND THE INTERNET

Cell phones or "mobiles" are now widespread and indispensable, even in the deepest countryside. Preferring to communicate voice-to-voice, Ethiopians are more likely to call rather than to "message." Similarly, they are more likely to prefer using instant message apps such as WhatsApp, Telegram, or Viber than to email. Indeed, foreigners are often disappointed when their emails to Ethiopian colleagues and friends remain unanswered. Cell phones are the most reliable means of contacting someone, although landlines continue to be used and offer a useful backup.

Smartphones are increasingly used, particularly in cities; and visitors using their own smartphones sometimes, but not always, find roaming facilities work for them. Local SIM cards can be purchased

on production of a passport. Credit for cell phones and for internet connection by dongle is by means of standard priced cards that can be purchased in kiosks and from street vendors. The hidden number on these is then keyed into the phone or the dongle, but it is wise to have an Amharic speaker to hand as some instructions are given in this language. WiFi for residents can be purchased by visiting a local Ethio Telecom office and producing the necessary proof of address. Internet cafés are widely available in cities, and broadband available in big hotels. Ethiopia's Internet domain is ".et."

Both cell phone service and Internet are controlled by Ethio Telecom, which has the ability to close down services, such as SMS, in national emergencies. Network problems in mountainous areas may also prove a frustration, as might frequent congestion on the system, making connections or downloading very slow at times.

The Internet, for those fluent in English, has opened Ethiopia to the world. As well as being used for information gathering, the Internet is used for expressing opinions. There are numerous political websites both hostile to the government and supportive of it, and a number of them use extremely abusive language. Opposition sites are often censored.

POSTAL SYSTEMS

The main global courier services operate very efficiently in Ethiopia. Parcels can be delivered or collected either from a building or from the relevant company's offices around Addis Ababa. Using a courier has become the preferred means by businesses for sending tangible items.

The post office, or Posta Bet, is still a venerable institution that delivers letters efficiently and cheaply to P.O. boxes in post offices throughout the country, although not to domestic addresses. Their post boxes are painted yellow and are found outside post offices. To rent a P.O. box, you will need to pay a small annual sum of money, in return for which you will be given your own key to a specific numbered box, from which you collect your own letters. If you receive a parcel, a note will be left in the box.

CONCLUSION

Ethiopia's diversity makes generalization extremely difficult. It is a nation comprising several nations; it is at once African and Middle Eastern; it is both traditional and modern; it has fast-moving cities with the latest gadgets, and rural areas set in a time warp. Underlying its various cultures, however, is a deep awareness of their shared history, which is a source of pride and which contributes to a sense of unity and nationhood.

If national character can be generalized then the Ethiopians are proud, sophisticated, and courteous, yet have a strong sense of their own moral superiority. They are a nation of individualists, making them superb athletes, but not necessarily team players. Lovers of systematic government and methodical bureaucracy, Ethiopians also show great creativity when a problem presents itself.

If you show respect for their culture and earn their trust, you will find that in an Ethiopian there is always an intelligent partner who is willing to look at problems in a new way, who is both a hardworking colleague and a loyal friend.

FURTHER READING

Reference

Cheru, Fantu; Cramer, Christopher; Oqubay, Arkebe (eds). *The Oxford Handbook of the Ethiopian Economy*. Oxford: OUP, 2019.

Archaeology

Phillipson, David W. *Ancient Ethiopia. Aksum: Its Antecedents and Successors*. London: British Museum Press, 1995.

Church

Binns, John. *The Orthodox Church of Ethiopia. A History*. London, New York: IB Tauris, 2016.

Fiction

Verghese, Abraham. *Cutting for Stone*. New York: Penguin Random House, 2010.

Gibb, Camilla. *Sweetness in the Belly*. Canada: Heinemann, 2006.

Mengiste, Maaza. *The Shadow King*. New York: W.W. Norton & Co., 2019.

Laird, Elizabeth; Yosef Kebede. *When the World Began: Stories Collected in Ethiopia*. Oxford: Oxford University Press, 2000.

Geography and Travel

Koehler, Jeff. *Where the Wild Coffee Grows*. USA: Bloomsbury, 2017.

Marsden, Philip. *The Chains of Heaven: An Ethiopian Romance*. London: HarperCollins, 2005.

Thesiger, Wilfred. *The Danakil Diary: Journeys through Abyssinia, 1930–34*. London: Flamingo, 1998.

History

Henze, Paul B. *Layers of Time: A History of Ethiopia*. New York: Palgrave Macmillan, 2004.

Zewde, Bahru. *A History of Modern Ethiopia 1855-1991*. Oxford: James Currey, 2002.

Pankhurst, Richard. *The Ethiopians: a History*. Oxford: Blackwell, 1998.

Rankin, Nicholas. *Telegram from Guernica: The Extraordinary Life of George Steer, War Correspondent*. London: Faber, 2003.

Biography

Edemariam, Aida. *The Wife's Tale*. London: HarperCollins, 2018.

Asserate, Asfa-Wossen. *King of Kings. The Triumph and Tragedy of Emperor Haile Selassie I of Ethiopia*. London: Haus Publishing, 2015.

Marsden, Philip. *The Barefoot Emperor*. London: Harper Press, 2007.

Natural History

Redman, Nigel; Stevenson, Terry; Fanshawe, John. *Birds of the Horn of Africa*. Princeton: Princeton University Press, 2009.

Sebsebe Demissew; Inger Nordal; Odd E. Stabbetorp. *Flowers of Ethiopia and Eritrea: Aloes and Other Lilies*. Addis Ababa: Shama Press, 2010.

Sebsebe Demissew; Phillip Cribb; Finn Rasmussen. *Field Guide to Ethiopian Orchids*. London: Royal Botanic Gardens Kew, 2004.

Travel Guides

Phillips, Matt; Jean-Bernard Carillet. *Ethiopia and Eritrea Travel Guide*. Melbourne/Oakland/London/Paris: Lonely Planet Publications, 2017.

Briggs, Philip. *Ethiopia*. Chalfont St. Peter, Bucks., England: Bradt, 2019.

USEFUL APPS AND WEBSITES

Useful Apps

Deliver Addis
Food delivery service in Addis Ababa

EtCal
Keep track of Ethiopia's festivals, fasts, and feasts

Ethiopian Airlines
For booking flights and check-in

PoloTrip
Ride-hailing taxi service in Addis Ababa

RIDE
Ride-hailing taxi service in Addis Ababa

Telegram
Ethiopia's most widely used instant messaging app

ZayRide
Ride-hailing taxi service

Useful Websites

www.addisstandard.com
Independent news website

www.borkena.com
Canadian based Ethiopian news service

www.thereporterethiopia.com
Weekly independent newspaper available free online

www.facebook.com/linkupaddis
Monthly online magazine for cultural events and news

www.ethiopianbusinessreview.net
Monthly business magazine (printed version available)

PICTURE CREDITS

Cover image: *Timkat Festival in Addis Ababa Ethiopia*. © iStock

Canva Photos: pages 28 by Dereje Belachew; 78 by Sergey; 88 by wilpunt; 180 justinfoster.

Pixabay Photos: page 77 by Limboko.

Unsplash Photos: pages 16 Erik Hathaway; 84, 110 by Gift Habeshaw; 118 by Matthew Spiteri; 167 kaleab.

Creative Commons Attribution-Share Alike 2.0 Generic license: 12, 14, 15, 23, 25, 26, 48, 53, 54, 70, 83, 90, 99, 100, 103, 108, 116, 125, 128, 129, 140, 178 © Rodd Waddington; 21 © Bernard Gagnon; 31 © Classical Numismatic Group; 41 © swiss-image.ch/Photo by Monika Flueckiger; 58 © Stijn Debrouwere; 68 © Richard Stupart; 70, 106 © Jasmine Halki; 102, 132, 148 © Ninara; 107, 127, 154 © Ian Swithinbank; 135 © A. Davey; 145 © Fran Villena; 147 © David; 162 © Andrew Moore; 177 © International Trade Centre; 187 © Jessica Lea/Department for International Development; 189 © Terje Skjerdal; 191 © Beyond Access.

Creative Commons Attribution-Share Alike 3.0 Unported: 7 © TUBS

Public Domain: pages 36, 38.

INDEX